FINALLY

A SURRENDER TO AUTHENTICITY

FREE

SETH SHOWALTER

Austin,
Be Real. Be True.
Be You!
Seth Showalter

Copyright © 2023 by Seth Showalter
First Edition

Cover Design by Rica Cabrix & Keith Giles
Interior Layout by Matthew J. Distefano

ISBN 978-1-957007-81-6

Published by Quoir
Chico, California
www.quoir.com

First and foremost, I dedicate this book to my brother. Over the years, my brother has served as a guiding light as I've explored my own journey of self-acceptance. I wouldn't be the man I am today or had the courage to write this book if it weren't for him. My brother has spent many hours listening to me ramble and stumble my way forward, showing grace, kindness and love.

As a first-time author, I would be remiss if I didn't also dedicate this book to my incredible editor, Crystal Kuld. She took on the massive project of working through a 300-page journal and working alongside me to produce the book that you hold in your hands. This book would not exist if it weren't for her guidance, patience, and impeccable editorial skills. Crystal took my experience and crafted my voice in a way I'll forever be grateful.

PREFACE

I HAVE DONE MY best to maintain the integrity of this journal from my time I spent at a gay conversion program in 2012. In order to respect the program's anonymity I will refer to it as NH for the remainder of this book. I have made changes to grammar, syntax, and overall flow of the original text, but many imperfections remain.

I have omitted days and portions of days from this journal to save my readers from the more tedious and repetitive aspects of the time I spent at NH. Otherwise, the portions from my journal used in this book remain the same as when I first wrote them.

Reader, take note: a stay at a residential facility is not always full of the drama, excitement and adventure that fictional stories typically contain (Here's looking at you, "Girl, Interrupted," and "One Flew Over the Cuckoo's Nest"). I was often bored, homesick, and depressed. I spent days doing little outsiders might consider "interesting". As a result, this book may not contain all the titillating and salacious episodes you might anticipate. My aim is to provide an authentic and realistic look into what I went through. What I went through was not always incredibly dramatic. My ultimate aim is to help others understand the emotional and spiritual repercussions of a Christian attempting to convert from being gay to straight.

———•◦•———

Most names of individuals mentioned in this book have been changed, unless these individuals have specifically provided consent for their name to be used. This was done to protect the identities of people involved. I have also omitted names of locations to provide the greatest anonymity possible.

LIST OF MOST INDIVIDUALS IN MY STORY

(The majority of names have been changed - Names used with permission when not):

<u>College:</u>

Justin: Friend
William: Campus Crusade Leader
Michael: Friend
Ethan: Friend
Alan: Campus Crusade Leader
Elizabeth: Friend
Sarah: Friend
Davis: Military Friend

<u>Family:</u>

Father
Mother
Brother
Billy: Cousin (Dad's Side)
Jeremy: Cousin (Dad's Side)
Kelly: Aunt (Dad's Side)

Staff:

Katherine: CEO and Counselor
Christopher: CEO's Husband / Co-leader
Matthew: Counselor
David: Counselor
Gavin: Counselor
Jack: Counselor
Jackie: Spiritual Counselor (contract employee)
Bob: Pastor / Counselor

Residents at NH:

Kevin
Marvin
Alex
David
Frank
William
Ron

Other:

Eric, Staff Co-worker from Youth Residential Program in College
Jeremiah, Older classmate from School
Ethan, Peer from Campus Crusade for Christ
Knives, Peer from College
Laura, High School Classmate
Mark, High School Spiritual Mentor and Mortician

INTRODUCTION

THE FOLLOWING INTRODUCTION IS an overview of my story from childhood until my days in a gay conversion program. Introductions often feel tedious and boring—like a mere formality. In my story however, the introduction is critical to understanding my history—who I am, what I have been through, and what led me to the decision to pursue conversion therapy. I therefore humbly ask the reader to take their time in reading the following pages. By neglecting to read this introduction, you will not have a clear understanding of what was really happening behind the scenes of (and prior to) my story.

In talking about my background, of course I should start with a brief overview of my childhood relationship with my parents. I will start out by stating that overall I have had an exceptionally positive familial experience. Compared to so many others, I consider myself blessed. I was born into a conservative Christian family. My two loving parents nurtured and taught me the fundamentals of life, instilling within me a knowledge of the difference between right and wrong. My parents held strong moral and religious convictions. These convictions significantly influenced my childhood life and worldview. Their guidance further laid the foundation for my own strong spiritual commitments throughout adolescence. Examples of childhood and adolescent behaviors instilled and encouraged by my parents included following the rules, never falling out of line. I did not drink or smoke prior to college. My graduating class nominated me "Most Likely to Become a Pastor."

In addition to my parents' influence over my moral and religious convictions, I experienced a life-altering event at age six. I was in a serious car accident which had lasting physical and psychological repercussions. This incident occurred on Thanksgiving morning that year.

I was riding to my grandparents' house in a small pickup truck with my sixteen-year-old cousin. My grandparents' home was located on a hill, and near their house was a nasty blind spot on the passenger side. Drivers approaching this area had to turn as quickly as possible to avoid an accident. In this instance, my cousin used his turn signal and waited a second too long before turning. Due to the delay, a car coming over the hill hit my side of the truck. The crash rendered me unconscious with multiple injuries. I had to be life-flighted to a larger hospital. The wreck placed me in a coma for six days, and the doctors diagnosed me with a traumatic brain injury (TBI). My TBI resulted in difficulty with processing information, impulsivity such as making irresponsible financial decisions, and seizures later in life (first onset, Christmas Day of 2013). These challenges intensified the already difficult parts of growing up.

Due to the physiological and psychological effects of the TBI my elementary, middle, and high school years were particularly hard for me. My cousins attended a nearby school. Due to the amount of rejection and emotional turmoil I'd been facing at my local school, my Aunt offered to let me live with her. However, my parents decided that I would stay with them, and I continued going to school in my hometown (their argument being the school's exceptional educational record). I struggled to fit in and often found myself the center of jokes. I had a tough time forming meaningful friendships with my peers, and invitations to parties or events were rare. My struggles with making friends and lack of approachability were related (at least in part) to the injuries I'd sustained in the accident. My TBI had altered my perception of reality and impacted my ability to appropriately respond to social situations. There were times I would hide at my locker in the hallway while my peers congregated together.

My mother was a special education aid and librarian at my school. This meant she was in the school building whenever I was. She was a constant witness to my traumatic school experiences. This sharedness and babying I got because of the car accident, in combination with my tender spirit, has always kept me in a close relationship with my mother—one I might even call codependent.

One of my parents' solutions to my social-emotional difficulties at the time was for me to participate in athletics. My school had an exceptional educational record but there was an unspoken rule that in order for students to really gain acceptance they must participate in sports. I can remember my parents comparing me to my more athletically gifted classmates (and even cousins) saying "If only you could enjoy sports like 'so-and-so' you would fit in." At their urging, I found myself in the position of junior high football manager in middle school. Later, in high school, I ran cross country because all the Christian kids did. When I say I ran cross country, I mean exactly that. I finished the races, but usually in last place. I did my best but was not a gifted athlete. At one home meet my junior year, I finished the race only to discover my entire team had already left. I was so slow *my own team* was unwilling to wait and watch me finish. Upon hearing about this incident, my father was outraged. In a way this was cathartic, because I felt like my father finally understood how difficult athletics and socializing with peers was for me. One sport I *did* enjoy was golf. I was decent at the game, and liked how I could spend time outside in nature.

Despite my social and athletic difficulties I did find an extracurricular activity that *was* within my interests. That activity was Forensics. In most people's minds Forensics refers to crime scene investigations. Forensics at my school though, consisted of writing and acting competitions. Another student named Kyleigh and I would do storytelling and duet acting. For storytelling, I would memorize a children's book, then perform the book back with distinct voices for all the different characters. For duet acting, Kyleigh and I would memorize short plays and then act those out by playing the different characters. We competed in regional competitions against neighboring school districts and were quite successful. We frequently won third place or better in these events. My parents supported my endeavors in Forensics. My father went as far as to become a judge at some of these competitions. I share all of this to say that while I felt inadequate when it came to sports, my parents were always supportive of me, regardless of my athletic prowess. They attended my events, volunteered to coach and judge, and encouraged me in what I enjoyed doing.

My parents were not the only family members near me. I have a brother who is seven years older. Growing up my brother and I were never that close emotionally speaking. This distance was due in part to our age difference. When he was a senior in high school I was still in elementary school. The fallout from my car accident had impacted my relationship with my brother in that I quickly became the center of my parents' attention. My parents coddled me, but not my brother. Things were not exactly "even" affection and attention-wise, and this disproportionate focus on me created frequent tension between us. My brother often felt as though he was getting short changed. For example, my parents would step in to give me financial assistance but then would not do so for my brother. As we have gotten older, we have worked through our past, but growing up it was a thing that kept us distant.

Despite our emotional distance my brother and I both turned out to be gay. With my brother being seven years older than me he was obviously the first to come out of the closet. In the summer of 2008, having just graduated from high school, I worked in North Carolina at a Christian Camp for boys. On my drive from Missouri to the camp I stopped to see my brother who was living in Illinois at the time. While he was away at work during my visit (and as any good brother would do), I found myself snooping through my brother's personal computer. I learned from this covert investigation that my brother was gay. I previously had no clue about his sexuality. While I had dabbled in sexual contact with a peer from school I had not yet come to terms with my own sexuality. Upon discovering my brother's secret I found myself in a state of surprise, shock, confusion, and guilt. I was told by friends and fellow church members that God saved me from the car accident for a "special reason" I had not yet discovered. Learning my brother was gay made *me* feel even more pressure not to be gay.

When my brother came home from work that day you could tell he immediately knew I had something by merely seeing the look on my face. I am not proud of myself now, but I decided it was my job to pressure my brother to come out to my parents later that summer while we were on a family vacation. My brother, parents, and I took this vacation at a Lake resort. It was mostly a wonderful and relaxing time. There was little arguing, and everyone mostly got along. One of the nights we were together on this trip felt like it was the right time for my brother to come out to my parents. I signaled this by giving him a wink. I then led the conversation by asking my brother if there was anything he needed to tell my parents. With my prompting my brother shared how he had experienced same-sex attraction for some time. My brother claimed he had been intentionally distant from our family for fear of being found out. He had felt there would be potential consequences from my parents such as financial or emotional cutoff. Upon hearing my brother's revelation, my parents did shed tears, however they did not cut my brother off. Instead, they stated that while they did not agree with the gay lifestyle, their love for my brother would never change. Looking back, I feel guilty for pressuring my brother into doing something he was not ready to do on his own. However, I felt my brother had been smart in waiting until he had graduated from his master's program before coming out to my parents. In doing so, he would have been able to survive if my parents had retaliated by financially cutting him off.

After we got back from this eventful vacation, my parents began the emotional journey of coming to terms with my brother's sexuality. They attempted to avoid showing their negative emotions to my brother and me, but it was evident they were experiencing a crisis of faith. I often found my mom sitting and crying in various rooms in our home. Looking back, it was likely my mother wondered what she had done wrong—how she had failed my brother as a parent. She once said that after all the trouble my brother and I had experienced in high school, she had expected daughters-in-law and grandchildren as a reward. All her friends were enjoying their growing families, and she ended up with a gay son. I once heard her tell my brother that if she were in my brother's shoes, she would never have burdened her parents with this information. After hearing her say this, I knew I could never disclose my own sexual struggles until I was straight.

My dad's response was more practical than my mother's. He was concerned that if my brother's sexuality were to become public knowl- edge, he could lose business as a salesperson. My brother's coming out challenged the foundation of what my dad believed to be true. Looking back, I know that my mother felt that she had been over-enmeshed, and my father felt that he had been too emotionally distant.

Due to my parents' struggle with accepting my brother's sexuality, both my brother and I encouraged my parents to pursue counseling to work through their feelings of failure. For unknown reasons, however, my parents were resistant to seeking emotional help. Overall, my parents' reluctance to talk through these issues made reaching acceptance more difficult. I remember feeling it was my responsibility to make my parents happy. To make them happy, I felt pressure to be straight, I had to get married, and I had to have kids. I had to be in the ministry, not just because I felt the calling to do so, but also to help bring my brother back to the Lord. Through all of this, I had a deep conviction that my parents could not know of my struggle with sexuality. I can remember feeling like the world was on my shoulders and that I could not do anything about it.

Accepting my brother's sexuality also provided me with a means to hide from concerns with my own sexuality. Part of why I have always found sexuality so confusing is that my first attraction to men began around the same time I was experiencing a profound sense of rejection from my male peers. I presented as heteronormative throughout elementary school and much of middle school. An example of this entails Grand Oaks Church Camp which I would attend during summers through adolescence. This was a cherished week for me as a child as it provided me with an escape from the real world. It also provided me with a plethora of opportunities to flirt with girls, and I took advantage of these opportunities. I can remember how I would compete with my cousins to see who could attract the most girls. We would each pick a picnic table in front of the dining hall and whoever got the most girls to sit with them won. While my cousins, Billy, and Jeremy, were able to attract girls with good looks and their musical abilities via guitar, I would engage the females around me with a smile and stimulate intellectual conversation. It turned out I had a bit of a following. I do not think it would be fair to say I was *attracted sexually* to women at this time, but I *was* attracted to the attention they gave me. Camp was an opportunity to get it.

In addition to the escape Grand Oaks provided, another reason I loved it so much was the opportunity it provided me to grow closer to God. I was raised in an evangelical church, and my faith had always been important to me. My family attended a small church thirty minutes south of my hometown. This church was run by a large number of family members on my father's side. I accepted Christ into my heart at an early age and can remember being baptized in a lake in front of my entire family and church family.

Due to never having fit in at my school, my time at church became a haven, even at an early age. I was frequently at church two to three times a week. For example, my Aunt Kelly, who was very instrumental in various children's ministries in our church, was a positive influence in my life. She encouraged me by involving me in plays she directed and would even cast me in lead roles. This was a stark contrast to the rejection I experienced at school. I would also sing solos at church and can remember singing "No Turning Back" on stage with my dad in front of the congregation.

As I entered my teen years, my relationship with Christ became a deeper source of strength and refuge. The message from my car wreck regarding "being saved for a reason" became something I grabbed onto early on in my faith. It not only served as a source of encouragement, but also a point of contention. As I entered my teen years and began to experience same-sex attraction, I could only rationalize that these feelings were part of the devil's plan to thwart God's mission for my life. If God had truly "saved me for a reason," why would he have me struggle with something that would "send me to hell?" It did not make sense and therefore, must have been an attack by the Devil.

I feel I did not undergo a "typical" gay experience in that I did not come to recognize my same-sex desires until later in adolescence, around age fifteen or sixteen after a male peer hit on me. This specific incident took place when I was working a summer job at one of those big pop-up tent fireworks stands while in high school. Another kid worked with me. He was a few years older but went to the same high school. This young man was popular and was successful at sports. Through working together, we became friends. Though it seems ridiculous now, having dealt with rejection and disdain from other males for so long, I began craving the attention and acknowledgment this popular guy gave me. One night at work, we were sitting on top of the tent, watching to ensure the fireworks stand was not being robbed. I do not recall the topic of conversation, but I do remember there was a lot of sexual tension in the air, and this felt new and exciting. I had not done anything or said anything to encourage this tension, and had not made any physical advances, but I certainly wasn't discouraging the electricity between us. At one point, without warning and without my asking, my friend reached over and grabbed my crotch.

This singular incident of sexual contact was a turning point for me in that I became acutely aware of my attraction to other males. I was not only being accepted but being given sexual gratification by someone who held social capital. This incident led to more sexual encounters, some of which included other friends of my coworker's.

Looking back at this experience now, I have found myself asking significant questions. Was this normal adolescent sexual experimentation or a form of sexual abuse? I had never asked to be touched. The truth remains, however, that there was an undeniable sense of mutual attraction that served as an invitation, as well as a natural progression of the way things were heading that night. I *do not*, however, believe that this one night's experience made me gay. It did serve as an opportunity for me to explore my sexual desires.

Having received male acceptance, but still feeling guilty about same-sex attraction, I did take a swing in the heterosexual dating world in high school. Jennifer and I met when we were teenagers at Grand Oaks Church Camp and remained friends over the years. We had always been close, and she was someone I regarded with high esteem. In fact, I would go as far as to say that I was at one time emotionally in love with her in high school. Our relationship was rooted in mutual respect, as well as our belief in Christianity. Our belief system tightly tied us together, but there was never any physical intimacy other than an occasional kiss. I never felt tempted to do more. I secretly hoped God would ignite a physical desire for intimacy with my girlfriend, but these desires never emerged.

Instead, my same-sex desires had continued to grow after that one night at the fireworks stand. I did not immediately connect these actions with homosexual behavior, but rather connected them to male intimacy and feelings of acceptance. In other words, I had engaged in homosexual activity but hadn't consciously acknowledged it as such. It was not until a third sexual partner was pulled into the mix that red flags started to flare, and I started to connect the dots. As these dots connected, I entered my own crisis of faith and identity, leaving me terrified.

I did not speak a word of my same-sex attraction to my family (or anyone else for that matter) for a few years. Instead, I got in my car and frequently drove to my small church. There I would fall face-first before the altar, begging God for help. I can remember crying my eyes out, pleading with God to do something, to change me, to fix me, to make things so that I would like girls like all the other men I knew.

The first person to whom I disclosed I thought I was gay was my high school spiritual mentor Mark. Mark worked as a "Christian Navigator"

(the Navigators are a worldwide Christian parachurch missionary organization whose goal is spreading the gospel) and was a very fundamental
type of Christian. He believed the Bible was perfect, having no faults, being one hundred percent true, no contradictions, etc., and the scriptures
provided a specific way to live. Upon learning of my same-sex attraction,
he provided a strong warning, stating the gay lifestyle was not something
in which I should dabble. He urged me to run away from this type of sin.

Because of the conviction that God had spared me for a yet-still-un-
known reason, I felt pressure to do something drastic about my emotional and sexual feelings toward men. There was a huge weight of
condemnation placed on homosexuality by the evangelical Christian
church, and I knew I was not going to be accepted as a fellow Christian
if I continued being gay. As a result, instead of starting college at a tradi-
tional four-year institution like my peers, I did something different. I had
started going to church at a megachurch an hour from my hometown
a couple times a week. I learned of an internship program offered for
people right out of high school. I jumped at this opportunity, as it served
as a way for me to show effort in doing something tangible to earn God's
intervention. I interned at this church for one year while taking general
education credits from a community college.

While in college and doing this internship, I continued to be involved
in the day-to-day events at my church. I attended church services on
Sunday, Wednesday, and Fridays. I was frequently at the church partic-
ipating in meetings and running Bible studies with students. Sundays
focused on the main service for the week. Wednesday nights were for
youth ministry, and on Friday nights they held an extra service for spiritual growth. My involvement at The Church became the center of my
world, and I formed strong relationships with several people in ministry
positions. On Friday nights after worship, the team would meet up after
and heavily drink alcohol. On one of these Friday drinking-nights, I
began talking with the worship leader. Our conversation led to physical intimacy, and we ended up having sex. Over my continued time
in ministry at this church, the worship pastor and I continued in our
relationship. Our sexual contact became a regular occurrence. With the
progression of this sexual relationship with the worship leader, came a
sense of mounting guilt and shame. I knew I was engaging in behaviors

that were sinful and wrong according to my faith tradition, and therefore kept concerns with my sexuality a secret from my family.

I began attending college at a nearby state university after my internship with the megachurch ended and was able to find housing with a guy from my hometown and two other guys in a house affiliated with Campus Crusade for Christ. Through this connection, I got involved in Campus Crusade, and worked to build a Christian community at the university. About two months into my first year at the University, I met someone by the name of Justin who was also involved in Campus Crusade. As fate would have it, we both struggled with same-sex attraction. We were both tempted and as a result, engaged in sexual activity with one another. Justin eventually shared our sexual encounter with his roommate, William. William and Justin were also involved in Campus Crusade for Christ, so they referred me to two ministry leaders for support: David for discipleship, and Alan for guidance. Knowing men whom I respected were now aware of my struggle, in this capacity, was humiliating and down-right embarrassing. With my "secret" being out in the open, I took steps in getting involved with Campus Crusade. I bought self-help Christian books geared towards changing one's sexuality and even attended a conference geared towards helping people overcome same-sex attraction. The books held valid points but, in the end, perpetuated my feelings of shame and guilt. I found this conference to be generic and awkward. While I took steps, I did not find such efforts to result in any real change or find them to be of significant benefit to me.

To contradict my homosexual tendencies and desires, I did attempt to pursue relationships with women in Campus Crusade. I remember thinking I had an attraction to a woman named Elizabeth, and then another named Sarah, but looking back, all I really felt was an affinity for their personalities. Nevertheless, I felt comfortable around Sarah, so I did tell her about my same-sex attraction. I remember being surprised with how blunt she was in her questions regarding what types of feelings I was having and gauging how serious I was about wanting to change. In the end, I felt I could trust her. However, the fact that my best female friend knew I liked men still scared me.

I sought discipleship with the Campus Crusade leader David. David challenged me to share my sin with others beyond those who already knew. He stressed the importance of bringing all sin into the light. He theorized that if I continue to keep my sin in the "dark," it would only grow and become a bigger problem. I struggled with this idea, fearing that sharing this sin would forever change people's opinion of me. I can recall feeling like I was on the edge of a cliff and people were asking me to jump.

As a result, I did "come out" and shared my sin struggle with two of my best friends in college at the time who were also involved in Campus Crusade: Michael and Ethan. Michael did not say anything, but I could not get Ethan to keep his mouth shut. He immediately went off about how this was only sin, and it did not make me any different. Hearing that said aloud from someone who I considered a best friend was immensely powerful. At the time, Ethan's generous and gracious response bothered me. I wanted him to freak out and cast judgment. I felt his judgment would make me feel better because it would prove that something was wrong with me. However, with Ethan being so understanding, I felt like I had been selfish and that this sin was indeed "my fault."

I also sought guidance in weekly meetings with a Campus Crusade leader by the name of Alan. Alan was a formerly professed gay man who reported having undergone gay conversion therapy. Through this therapy, he claimed he had found freedom from homosexuality. He was now married to a female and had children with her. Campus Crusade's leaders believed that due to Alan's ability to change, Alan was someone for me to emulate. He was living proof that homosexuality didn't have to be the answer. I was quite close to Alan for a while until one day when he provided a spiritual analysis of my life that was so full of judgment and off-center that I lost interest and grew quite cold toward him. In this analysis, Alan told me I knew about God and theology, but I had never allowed this information to touch my heart. He reported that he believed I did things to get noticed by peers and adults, and to receive acceptance. That was what my Christianity was, an attempt to get others to notice me. He called my desire to change and involvement in Campus Crusade combined with feelings of same-sex attraction hypocritical. He stated that I was living on a self-constructed throne and that I was not allowing Christ to have control over every aspect of my life. He was calling me a fraud, which was extremely harsh. I never really engaged with him again.

Interactions like these began to eat at me, and my internal conflict continued to intensify. One morning stands out in memory. I was sitting on the porch of the house I was living at with the guys from Campus Crusade. It was 6 am. I had not exactly slept. On the day prior I had attended a ministry meeting seeking to overcome their homosexual desires. After this class, I had purposely sought out a hook-up. I had no reason to do so, I wasn't even that aroused. I knew the consequences and I knew it was a sin. I engaged in the activity anyway. The shame and guilt washed over me, and I sat in my car crying and crying. I was empty. I was physically present, but my mind and spirit were not. I had become numb. After hooking up, I smelled like sex, so I just sat in my car and ended up studying in a parking lot instead of going home. Eventually I sat on the porch. I had been experiencing reality in something of a daze. People - Places - Events... Everything was moving around me. Life was happening but I was not present for it.

My second year at college, I moved in with two of the guys in the Social Work program (my major). My hope was that by removing myself from an ultra-Christian environment, I might find freedom from my internal conflicts. My roommates were both straight, but nice guys overall. I soon met one of the guys who lived next door to us named George. The first night George and I met, we were up all night talking. I ended up spending the night at his place.

My relationship with George progressed from there, and it was the definition of unhealthy. This was my first attempt at a real relationship, and I had no idea what I was doing. Every step of the way felt wrong because I knew that my faith said this relationship was sinful. I desperately wanted to be okay with who I was and to be free to explore my sexuality. However, shame and guilt were still strong forces in my life—so strong that I sought to numb this with alcohol and marijuana, which George also enjoyed. Over time, our relationship began to center around these substances. There was rarely a time when George and I were together when we were not under the influence in one way or the other. In addition to the alcohol and marijuana use, George and I also both had very high sex drives. Feeding this sexual appetite became a common distraction—Sex. Drugs. And Alcohol.

My parents were aware of my so-called friendship with George. I tried to make George sound like a positive force in my life. However, George's aspirations were quite different from my own. While I was in school pursuing an undergraduate degree in Social Work, George had only graduated from high school and was not pursuing higher education. There is nothing wrong with not pursuing higher education, but George's lack of ambition was evident. He worked at a hardware store and lived with his roommates. I started working in direct care with at-risk youth and lived with other social workers. Our chosen paths were different. The only things we really had in common were that we were both gay and that we both were using drugs and alcohol as a way of numbing our own psychological distress.

The closer George and I grew, and the more difficulties I faced with my ministry with Campus Crusade, it became more challenging to keep the secret of my sexuality from my family. I initially came out to my brother since he was already out and might be able to give me advice. I recall we were driving somewhere when I told him. I came out by asking what would happen if I was the same as him? What if I had the same type of attraction as him? I vividly remember my brother's immediate reaction which was "I'm the first-born child, you must do what mom and dad think is best." He said this mostly as a joke, but the sentiment was real. I was deeply involved in the faith, and he had already come out of the closet, therefore following the already established conventions of our religious parents made sense.

In 2010, I starred in the Shakespeare Play "Othello" with a local community theater. After one of the performances, I came out to my mother. I recall feeling compelled to finally tell her the truth. We met at a nearby parking lot after the play, and I joined her in her vehicle. I shared that there was something that I needed to tell her. Based on how I started this conversation, my mother must have had an inclination that this was serious as she immediately asked me if I struggled with the same thing as my brother. I felt I had kept my homosexual tendencies at bay quite well, but my mother must have had an inkling. Through my tears I remember shaking my head, "No" and then answering, "Yes." I tried to smooth the news by explaining that while I had same-sex attraction, I knew it was wrong and I did not want to live that way.

After sharing this information, my interactions with my parents became a bit awkward. Since they were now aware of my sexual feelings towards men and how I did not want to be that way, keeping things from them felt counter-productive. Sharing personal information became the rule rather than the exception. It was as if talking had opened the flood-gates and there was nothing I could not share.

An example of the oversharing is that I would share intimate details about my friendship with George with my parents—mostly my mother, who would then relay this information to my father. They learned all about George, both the positive and the negative aspects of our relationship. They became well acquainted with his drinking habits and they were well informed about my feelings about him. They knew all the details about my difficulties with Campus Crusade for Christ—how I felt rejected by the organization and leaders. They became well informed of my relational difficulties in friendships, including my bouts of loneliness. Given all of this, I also became transparent regarding my alcohol and marijuana use. My substance use led me to often make unwise financial decisions and my parents would always have to step in and help me out. To put it simply, there was nothing that my parents did not know.

I graduated from college in December of 2011. After graduation, an impromptu intervention of sorts convened in the basement of my parents' house that next weekend. I honestly do not remember how the conversation started but I do remember crying and begging them for help. My brother was present. The thought that kept running through my mind was to ask that they throw me in a room, lock the door, and throw away the key until I would be able to walk away a changed person. Let me make this clear. My parents *did not* force me into any type of conversion therapy program. They made no ultimatums that I had to undergo this treatment or suffer loss of relationship or financial support. I had requested this help. My brother tried to talk my parents out of going along with my plan. He was concerned about the psychological damage conversion therapy could cause. Given how well-informed my parents were in my difficulties with relationships, with substances, and with the inner turmoil I had been experiencing, they wanted to support me.

It did not take them long to find a program. I was not part of the process. My parents were tasked with finding a program that would address substance use and same-sex attraction under my father's insurance. Therefore, they did not send me to the standard gay conversion therapy program. Instead, they found a small Christian residential substance use treatment facility in California called NH. Being a Christian-run facility, the staff believed that if God had the power to heal the alcoholic, He had the power to heal the homosexual. My parents were convinced to send me after my interview process with the co-owner Katherine. Katherine was truly a unique individual and communicated in a way that spoke directly to the soul. She won me over immediately. So after a conversation with her, I was convinced to go.

I want my story to serve as a guidepost and warning to those who may be in a comparable situation. After reading parts of my story, my hope is that you will be able to learn from my experiences and grasp the changes that took place during my stay. It is my desire that this book will help and support other individuals who feel compelled to try to change their sexuality for religious reasons.

DAY 1

I have made the decision to enter this treatment program for several reasons: I have been living a homosexual lifestyle with frequent one-night stands and hookups with other men. This has led to an extreme sense of guilt, which has caused me to drink excessively and frequently get high on weed (which consequently leads me to make poor decisions in further hookups and one-night stands). I feel I am living a life of constant internal conflict, guilt, and confusion, and am miserable as a result. I want to have fulfilled relationships with myself, my family and with God. But I also know I am frustrated by the conflicting messages I get about the Bible, what "Truth" is, and whether being gay is "sinful" depending on who I ask. All I know is I am unhappy and feel I have not been living the right way.

I want to feel good in my own skin. I don't want to continue being at war with who I am. Was I born gay? Can my homosexuality change? Am I truly a Christian? What factors are behind all these problems in my relationships? Am I strong enough to live a life of integrity? These are all questions that I would like answered and why I've found myself in California.

1

It is hard to place a value judgment on whether my introduction to NH was good or bad. It just was. I did not know what I had signed up for and was walking into an unknown world. A therapist could have walked me through locked doors, and I would not have been alarmed. Okay, maybe I would have been alarmed, but you get my point. I did not know what I was getting myself into and was in for the ride. The fact that I was entering into a program to change my sexuality had deeply impacted me, making me feel I was doing something incredibly drastic. I had not yet publicly come out of the closet and was going into this intensive program trying to change the very nature of who I was. I was in an uncharted realm and did not know what to expect.

> *After the tour, an employee named Gavin searched through all my stuff. I was an idiot and left the receipt of the airport "rum and coke" in the book I had been reading. Gavin had to have caught that embarrassing piece of evidence. I was informed I am not allowed to have my phone, iPod, camera, or the book I've been reading. Gavin gave a rundown of the house rules and had me fill out loads of paperwork.*

The staff initially presented themselves as kind and caring. They treated me the same as one of their typical substance-use clients. However, given that the facility consisted of multiple converted homes, it did not have a particularly professional feel. It felt more like the location for a retreat. Most of the staff provided a calm and welcoming presence. Gavin, however, was not friendly. It makes sense that he, responsible for providing the house rules and guidelines, had to come across as a hard ass. However, this was not a great first impression for someone who was there to change his sexuality.

> *Upon arriving at NH, I was shown that there are two homes for residents. The main house, where I'm staying, is for*

clients who are engaged in the intensive residential program. The second house is a sober living home - providing a step-down program. The homes are located in two separate cul-de-sacs. I am living in the main house and have a room all to myself. There are four other residents. I'm the youngest of the group and staff. The house and its rooms are extremely nice. It's incredible I'm living in an actual house to receive the help I need. I'm still processing the fact I'm in an actual residential treatment program. The fact I will be living here for three months hasn't yet sunk in.

In my ten-plus years' experience in the field of mental health professions, I can say that across-the-board residential treatment facilities vary in numerous ways. Some facilities are specialized and are state of the art, having multiple amenities. Others are "mom and pop" setups like NH. Therefore, while I was surprised that NH consisted of homes instead of a quote on quote "facility," I was not too surprised. Would I have felt more comfortable in an established facility over a big home in California? Probably. It is honestly hard to know.

DAY 2

DAY TWO STARTED WITH me celebrating how amazing the program was:

> *I absolutely love it here. It is amazing. It appears every day will be full of Bible studies with treatment material sprinkled in. All of our meetings, groups, and studies are focused on God. I can be honest, I don't feel like I have to pretend or act like someone I am not. I haven't experienced this authenticity since I was back in my childhood church. I can already feel myself growing closer to God in a way I know will strengthen me. There is Hope. That's right: HOPE. It's like a fresh breath of air.*

The day ended with me asking God to speak, wondering what I had gotten myself into.

> *I was left alone outside with my thoughts. What the heck am I doing here? I'm experiencing two opposite extremes. On the one hand, I feel my problems aren't as severe as the others' here. But then I also fear I'm too messed up for help and my problems are too complex. I'm terrified of the guys knowing the real reason I am seeking treatment. I walked around outside for thirty minutes. I sat down on the basketball court outside and stared up at the stars. I confessed my sin, my pride, my manipulation, my arrogance, and my brokenness. I then became silent and asked God to speak. I*

neither felt nor heard anything. I heard myself think, "It's going to be okay. God has a plan. You are not alone." Were those my own thoughts or were they from God? How would I know the difference?

As I began this program, I felt an immense sense of powerlessness. This could have been intentional on the part of the NH Staff. When we are in a place of uncertainty, find ourselves out of our element, and do not know what to expect, people in positions of authority in these types of settings can take advantage to manipulate us. This was evident in Jackie and Alex's spiritual episode:

A group therapy session this evening appeared to have a spiritual impact on everyone here. A counselor named Jackie was facilitating. To get things started, Jackie began by reviewing the themes in a film that the other residents had recently watched. I was surprised by the apparent impact the themes of abandonment and grief had on the guys in the group. It was fascinating to hear their observations and feelings the movie brought out.

After the movie discussion, it came time for Alex's turn to share. At first, Alex seemed reluctant to speak from his heart, but Jackie was skilled at drawing him out. With Jackie's encouragement, Alex was able to discuss how the death of his mother when he was three left him feeling completely abandoned. Jackie pushed him further still. It's hard to explain, but as I watched and listened to Alex and Jackie's interaction, I was able to sense a spiritual energy in what was occurring. There was an almost palpable power in the air, and I felt like I could hear a pin drop. Alex explained that at age three his body and mind could not handle the pain of his loss and abandonment from his mother. As a result, he felt internally divided. He had lived his life up to this point a mere shell of a person. Listening to Alex tell his story, he seemed to be fighting tears with every ounce of his being. With Jackie's continued questioning, Alex began to break down and cry. Jackie challenged Alex to picture his mom lying in the hospital bed where she died. Anger and hatred seemed to well up from Alex, as he clenched his fists against the tears running down his face. Jackie asked him to picture Jesus in this memory at the hospital. She prayed Christ would open Alex's spiritual eyes, ears, and heart. Alex began to weep. He said Christ was there and was holding both him and his mother. When he was asked what he was experiencing at that moment, Alex said Christ told him to "let go." We watched Alex's demeanor completely transform from bitter and angry to relaxed and relieved.

Alex later shared how what he envisioned was not a mere personification nor his imagination. It had been the most real encounter with Christ he'd ever experienced. I shared how I had experienced something similar, but the emotional potency of that experience had faded over time. I encouraged Alex to write down everything he'd experienced. This was not a moment he would want to forget. I reminded Alex that God's glory is most satisfied when man is most weak, when man is weak Christ is strong.

When emotions are easily manipulated, we can be led to believe things we otherwise would not. Looking back at this experience ten years later, it is hard to determine what occurred from actual "spiritual forces" vs. the emotional maneuvering performed by the counselors.

I was already encountering a spiritual event where someone was actively addressing their past (but in a completely non-empirical way, i.e., a spiritual one). Having just graduated with a bachelor's degree in social work, Jackie's therapy approach seemed a bit out of the norm, if not unethical. Now, years later, I definitely *do not* regard Jackie's approach as ethical. However, this appeared to be a genuinely spiritual moment for Alex, evidenced by his emotional state. Alex would later go on to talk about this being the pivotal encounter through which he was able to find freedom from the trauma that had held him hostage for quite a long time.

DAY 3

I'm starting to feel inferior to another resident at NH named Marvin. I know Marvin is trying to be helpful, but he already corrected me on three chores he felt were not up to his standard this morning. It seems the only time he speaks to me is to tell me to do something or to correct me. I'm beginning to think I'm not liked by some of the others here, and to some extent, I can't fit in. I'm aware these feelings are not rational and I'm being overly self-conscious, but those characteristics are part of who I am.

THIS INTERACTION WITH MARVIN was the first negative exchange I experienced at NH. I already was deeply insecure and struggled to feel comfortable socializing with other men prior to the program. Once at NH, I felt a powerful sense of pressure to immediately fit in with the other residents. It was not just that they were the only people with whom I could socialize, but I was also the youngest of anyone there. I wanted to please Marvin and meet the facility's expectations. When I realized how lofty Marvin's standards of perfection were, not meeting those standards further enforced my own internal feelings of guilt, shame, and rejection. In my already-heightened emotional state, no form of criticism would have been well-received. Looking back, I think Marvin may have been hyper-focused on chores, knowing how Christopher typically reacted when things weren't done to his liking. While I was receiving his criticism with negativity, Marvin may have been doing what he could to protect me from Christopher's wrath.

Before going to an AA meeting, I lay in bed pondering my anger, fear, and anticipation. Anger because I am in this place to begin with and my mental health doesn't seem to be being considered (i.e., psychiatric medication). I fear I might not be fully committed or surrendering enough for God to work. I'm filled with anticipation, hoping God will do some miracle to make me straight. Given these perplexing emotions, I stayed quiet in the AA group tonight. When it came time for me to talk, I passed.

After attending a Christian AA meeting, I had a meeting with Gavin and shared some of my true feelings. First, I requested my parents be called so my antidepressants can be sent to the facility. Second, I addressed my concerns around the reason why I was at the facility versus the treatment I was receiving. I'm tired of being hyper-focused on Jesus. I have done the whole pray-the-gay-away thing for years and Jesus hasn't done anything. I may sound arrogant, but I feel my problems are too complex for this program.

Another weird component of this day was the Christian AA meeting. While I was in this program for substance use and sexual orientation change, my *primary* reason for being in this program was assistance in changing my sexuality. The staff required me to attend AA meetings and expected me to introduce myself, stating my specific addiction. How exactly should this have looked for someone who was addressing their being LGBTQIA+? At the time, I concluded my best strategy would be to just keep my mouth shut so I could process and create an appropriate response.

DAY 4

Christopher (the boss and Katherine's husband) was with us today. We had a short conversation which didn't go well. He wanted to understand why my moods were so back and forth and why I felt the need to be on psychiatric medication. I had to explain what it is like to experience major depressive disorder and why I find being on medication so important. I'm certain I came across as an asshole. I don't believe Christopher likes me. He wants me to take a day to assess my behavior before he calls home to have my psychiatric medications sent. I need my psychiatric medications damnit!

I FEEL I SHOULD address NH' reluctance to let me receive my psychiatric medication. Individuals with a fundamentalist mindset often feel psychiatric medications "dull" or "bury" feelings, preventing people from letting God do his work. However, as someone who had experienced a traumatic brain injury (and, really, this applies to anyone else with a diagnosed mental health disorder), NH's refusal and attempts to convince me to stop taking my medication was inconsiderate, unethical, and wrong. No one at the facility had any medical expertise qualifying them to make recommendations on any medication (let alone psychiatric meds), and this was completely out of line. Further, had the staff been

9

successful in convincing me to go off my medication, they certainly were not equipped, not having the training, to deal with the repercussions. I would have gone through some potentially significant withdrawal.

I had done all the praying, had done all the "spiritual formation" activities my church had told me to do, had asked God to take my depression away, time and time again. Saying God could solve my depression after I had asked Him to do so many times in the past without success was utterly presumptuous and disrespectful. The staff did not take my mental health seriously at all.

> *After evening church, we were given the rest of the night off. Things got better from here. Alex and I talked outside for quite a while. During our conversation, I finally got the courage to tell him the real reason I am here and the changes I hope to make. Alex did not appear surprised by this revelation, so maybe sharing with the group won't be such a bad experience after all. After this, my conversation with Alex went more smoothly. I realized I don't have to act or pretend around him. He actually cracked jokes about my situation. Surprisingly, he doesn't think I 'should' change and that I should just accept myself.*

As it was my primary reason for being at NH, coming out to the other residents was an obvious foregone conclusion. The conversation where I came out to Alex still proved to be a nerve-racking experience. Having finally shared the primary reason for my being there, though, a weight off my shoulders lifted, and I felt a significant sense of relief. I no longer needed to hide (at least from Alex, one person at NH I considered a peer). I was surprised at his response. I was expecting for him to be shocked. Alex had no idea NH offered gay conversion services and did not feel this was the approach I should be taking. Rather, Alex advocated for me accepting myself and even spoke to the loving nature of God. Ironic, eh?

DAY 5

God has a cruel sense of humor. He allowed my pride to swell up, but then Katherine, the CEO (and person who gets things done) at the facility showed up to meet with me. I will be having meetings with her every week. She pried into my struggle with homosexuality and asked me questions I have been unwilling to answer. We discussed so many things, I can't begin to write about them. I started my day off angry and resentful toward God, but after speaking with her, I had renewed hope and amazingly, a little trust in Him. She gave me a book on walking out of homosexuality. It feels good to finally be addressing my homosexuality. I've been waiting for this and I'm looking forward to delving into it.

Katherine also challenged my silence on personal issues in groups. She said the counselors will give me a few days to adjust, but if I don't open up soon, they are going to intervene and make me start talking about my issues.

Katherine isn't playing games—we talked for over an hour. She is going to force me to deal with God, which I haven't liked to do. I've become something of an expert at putting on a mask and pretending to be someone I'm not, especially in my relationship with Christ. There is a gap between the theology I have in my head and the life I live in my heart. Katherine is going to challenge me to bridge that gap which will not be easy.

I HAD AN AFFINITY for Katherine, partly because of her tender and warm-natured spirit. She presented a deeply knowledgeable and hyper-spiritualized persona. I felt I could immediately trust her because of the warmth and wisdom she exuded—the spiritual knowledge she seemed to possess. In a way, it felt as though she had magical powers, and miraculous things just happened around her. Since I was not aware of how the promised sexual orientation change would come to be, I viewed my work with her as mystical. Katherine told me I would be meeting with her privately to do intense work on sexual orientation change. It would require me to "face God," which caused me to feel encouraged. While I had some reservations, my own uncertainty of what this work would be like kept me hopeful.

An RN, not affiliated with NH, came to talk to us tonight about the effect of drugs on the brain. I found the group the RN led interesting on both an educational and intellectual level. However, it was much more than that for the rest of the guys. Not only did they all identify as alcoholics, but many admitted to being meth, heroine, and cocaine addicts. I suddenly felt I was sitting in a state hospital like the one I interned at last semester. How am I supposed to be relating, identifying, and growing in such an environment when my primary problem is homosexuality?

Since I asked to have my psychiatric medications shipped here, Christopher had the RN talk with me after the group ended. In order to justify my desire to take psychiatric medications, I had to explain my struggle with homosexuality. The nurse was shocked to hear I would want to change my sexuality. He asked why I am at a drug and alcohol treatment center to do so. His view was that I may be able to change, but the chances are not very high. This conversation has left me torn. I feel Christopher doesn't want me to take psychiatric medication because of the old conservative Christian narrative stating you don't need drugs because God is stronger. I am completely against this line of thinking regarding mental health. We would never say something like that to someone who was facing a cancer diagnosis. Mental health should be viewed as important as physical health. Jesus is not the answer to everything. The talk I had with the RN made me quite upset and confused. Why wasn't the RN on the same page as Christopher?

That Christopher had not vetted the RN's opinion on sexual orientation prior to my meeting with him was strange. It honestly seemed disorganized and beyond confusing as a person receiving treatment. From my present social work standpoint, this was unprofessional and bordered on unethical. From my current perspective, I understand the need to have me speak with a Registered Nurse (RN) regarding my medications; however, informing the RN why I was receiving treatment should have been a step to take prior to our meeting. As a licensed clinical social worker (LCSW), that would have been my recommendation. Not doing so put me, the client, in a tailspin of confusion, especially since the RN did not hold the same perspective as NH on changing sexual orientation.

Later, we had a group on "Every Man's Battle." The talk centered on masturbation and how to avoid lusting after women. "The boss" Christopher showed up and so did his friend. His friend went on a tirade about how the only way to conquer sexual sin is to analyze the intent of your heart and ask for the Holy Spirit to change it. The temptation will never go away (no shit Sherlock) but with the Holy Spirit's power we can turn away and avoid sin. Good stuff, but after talking to Katherine my emotions were shot. I wasn't too excited about the talk.

Christopher pressed me to share all this information [come out] in the morning group. He is going to be there, so I will have no choice in the matter. I shared my concern that the others might judge me. Christopher told me to 'trust him'. He then brought Kevin (another client) into my room. Christopher proceeded to have me tell Kevin about my homosexuality. My hands started sweating, my feet began shaking, and my words came out in a rush. I gave a short synopsis of my story. Kevin didn't know what to do and didn't seem to know why he had been asked to hear all this.

Christopher forcing me to come out to Kevin was an extremely uncomfortable experience. Christopher did not warn me. He simply brought Kevin into my room and initiated this conversation. At the time, I viewed Christopher's actions as a form of betrayal. While I now understand that Christopher intended to use this as an opportunity for "practicing coming out," he blind-sided me. I felt a major break in trust. At the very least, Christopher should have said this interaction was going to happen. He should have allowed me to choose someone with whom to practice coming out. He did not offer either option, this experience was forced upon me.

DAY 6

Christopher had us watch a video of a pastor speaking at a Christian college. The purpose of his speech was to argue that evolution was a lie, and the Earth is six thousand years old. This goes against scientific fact. Christopher believes him; however, I am not so easily persuaded. I feel being forced to watch this film attacked my intelligence. It's ignorant and I am not about to throw my intelligence under a bus and become ignorant as well. I imagine God is laughing, if not crying, by the stupidity and lack of faith in such sermons and beliefs.

———◦———

THAT A CHRISTIAN DRUG and alcohol rehab facility would require their clients to watch a video on evolution seemed a bit strange, especially since it had nothing to do with recovery. I would come to learn that the staff at NH needed activities to keep clients busy. If they could give an activity the "Christian" label, it would suffice, regardless of whether it had anything to do with recovery. I was being required to watch Christian propaganda having nothing to do with addiction or my sexual orientation change effort.

I need to learn to keep my mouth shut. As I've said before, NH is a little 'fundamental' in their understanding of Christian theology and doctrine. It's apparent the leaders operate the facility from a conservative perspective. NH also holds to the concept of The Rapture. After hearing about how we should be afraid of The Rapture too many times, I opened my mouth. I should probably have kept silent. Rapture theology isn't easily dismissed. I hope by offering my opinion I haven't lost ground or credibility in the house. I fear I have and may not be taken seriously.

For those who may not be familiar, The Rapture is an evangelical Christian theory asserting Christ's eventual return. According to Rapture Theory, when He returns, Christ will call up all His followers into the sky. He will take all the Christians to heaven and will leave all non-believers on Earth to fight a seven-year war. Although this belief has been around for more than one hundred years, it became re-popularized in the United States when the "Left Behind" series was published in the late 1990s and early 2000s. The books and their subsequent movies were based on passages of the Bible describing Christ coming back and his followers meeting him in the sky (such as referenced in Matthew 24).

We shared communion as a group. One of the counselors, Matthew, read a scripture from 1 Corinthians pertaining to communion. He then surprised me by saying the Lord had called him to wash the feet of someone in the group. Of course, to my dismay, I was the chosen one. I was wearing yellow socks. I also have somewhat deformed hammer toes. So much embarrassment. Having my feet washed by others was very humbling, but also powerful. However, I'm not upset. I am rather honored. Christopher also wanted to take part in washing my feet. Both Matthew and Christopher spoke very positive and uplifting words about God's love for me and plans He has for my life. After that, Hunter [a fellow resident] also wanted to wash my feet. That meant so much to me because Hunter already holds a special place in my heart. For him to get on his hands and knees to wash my feet, well, it was humbling. Hunter had Gavin read a scripture from Isaiah, which referred to God granting strength.

While this all meant a lot to me, receiving the foot washing was difficult. I have my doubts it was done with pure intentions. I fear the staff's motivation was to lessen my pride. I just have my doubts.

The foot washing exercise was powerful and very emotional for me. Looking back, my feelings about it are mixed. I suspect I may have been correct—that the foot washing was conducted (at least in part) to get me to fall in line with the program. At this point in my journey, I was rebelling against a lot of what NH represented. The foot washing felt intended to make me humbler and more compliant. I suspected Christopher may have planned this exercise, at least in part, to manipulate me. However, I also felt a genuine outpouring of care, compassion, and love from my fellow residents.

As I said in my journal, part of my difficulty in receiving the foot washing resulted from my own insecurity about the appearance of my feet. I am still very sensitive about them, and rarely allow others to see them to this day. This physical insecurity, mixed with reception of this act of service, made for a humbling experience. As of day six, I was not fully on board with the program, nor was I certain about making the changes the staff were telling me were necessary. This was likely evident to staff and clients alike. The foot washing could have been suggested as a way of getting me to fall in line. Looking back, I would not put anything past Christopher.

DAY 7

Christopher had us go serve and spend time with the home-less. We found a few people who were homeless living in tents near the freeway. To my surprise, Christopher allowed me to bring my camera. That seriously brightened my day, and I got some good shots.

Witnessing how the homeless live is always eye opening. A large percentage of the people we encountered here live in a community together. It was almost like a quietly existing city, unknown to most people. They live in tents and have their own societal norms, expectations, and rules. They've created their own world. I think this is fascinating. Humanity forms its own system of interactions and expecta-tions, even among the homeless. These individuals have instilled meaning in their lives and have constructed a community and operate as a family. It reminded me of the Apostle Paul in Acts and the beginning of The Church. Everyone shares freely among themselves.

WHILE MOST OF MY experiences at NH were less than uplifting (let alone inspirational), there were occasional events that were more pos-itive. The times I was able to spend serving the homeless proves as an example. In a way, these outings provided a sense of connection with the "real world" as well as my career choice of being a social worker. Having graduated with a bachelor's degree in social work just prior to entering this program, working with the homeless served as a bridge to what I really wanted to do with my life: serve. This type of activity drove home core messages of humility, service, and compassion.

> *Accepting my presence here has become a challenge. I don't feel my life has ever become completely unmanageable. Even with my sexual encounters, pervasive depression, and binging with alcohol and marijuana, I was able to graduate college with a 3.5 GPA and work twenty-five hours a week. Is a residential treatment facility really necessary? The staff here don't allow me to use the Internet, check my email, call my friends, or use my computer. I feel my rights have been stripped, but for what? So, I can somehow stop sexually acting out? Are these restrictions really required? It feels like running around a house four times and then entering through a basement window instead of walking through the front door, tiring and exhausting for no reason.*

At this point in the journey, I was living in a state of denial regarding the help I needed and the seriousness of my situation back home. Prior to entering this program, my life *had* become unmanageable. To be blunt, I had been out of control. I was drinking way more than I should have. I was making unwise decisions not only putting my own life in jeopardy, but also the lives of others. I would frequently drink shots during the week and would drink more heavily during the weekends. I was making unwise decisions. Since my sexuality was a major aspect of why I came to NH, I used it as a reason to not engage with other aspects of the treatment process. I did not want to explore issues that would reveal my weaknesses, particularly with alcohol and marijuana. I wanted to pretend substance use was not a primary concern and wanted to solely focus on my sexual orientation change. The substance use was a byproduct stemming from believing I was unacceptable before God. However, the program required vulnerability toward something I was not ready to admit to myself.

> *We had to 'super clean' the house today. I did what I normally do for my morning chores (patio and garage) and then proceeded to help Marvin clean the bathroom. I was later told I didn't do an acceptable job and Marvin had to pick up the slack. I felt bad about this because I haven't had to clean a bathroom this thoroughly in a long time.*

The rules put into place by Katherine and Christopher seemed very intense and harsh to me at the time. Truthfully, having just gotten an undergraduate degree and immediately entering treatment required a great deal of surrender. I was open to surrender, but at the same time, felt resistant. The rules and regulations were justifiable; however, the communication around said rules and regulations could have been managed differently. I constantly felt like I was in the dark or somehow in trouble while I was in the program.

DAY 8

I feel I'm growing rather cynical. I've been here an entire week and haven't learned a single practical skill for when I leave. I am not getting 'better,' or moving toward a change in sexuality. I am simply postponing life in the real world. I am beginning to feel I am being manipulated. The counselors/staff say the Holy Spirit is leading them, but it looks as if they are doing whatever they can to make more money. This becomes pretty clear when staff tell me, "I am meant to be here" or "this is the perfect place for you."

The material I'm doing with Katherine is helpful, but we are only going to meet once a week. I am going to have to endure class after class only to get one useful hour a week. I agree I should be receiving some form of help and therapy, but this program seems like a waste of time, effort and money.

Upon signing up with NH, I feel the staff made promises regarding me being able to change my sexual orientation. However, it did not appear the staff had a lot of experience managing these types of issues. NH was a substance use residential treatment facility, and they did not specialize in gay conversion therapy. The staff had been very adamant, however, that sexual orientation change was possible. Something I could not and still do not understand is how this change could have been possible with only one focused session a week with Katherine. If the facility took sexual orientation change so seriously (or had they known what they were doing), I feel they would have provided a more intensive approach. It is hard not to think my suspicion was correct. NH was in the business of making money.

The pressure to change is so overwhelming. I don't want to let my family down. Christopher saw my emotional state and challenged me to talk with him. Without fully processing ahead of time, all my fears, angers and concerns came rushing out. I believe my words offended Christopher. After this conversation, he told the other guys we would not be going to the beach this upcoming weekend as previously planned. It seems I have ruined everything for everyone. It's entirely my fault. Sharing my true thoughts with Christopher was the worst thing I could have done.

Christopher told me he feels there is dissention in the house and that it should be anointed. I was overcome with shame and guilt. The guys began praying over the house, but I slipped off to my room. At that moment, I wanted to run. Shame and guilt on top of an emotional breakdown are a little much to bear. I wanted out of here. However, since running away wasn't an option, I further humiliated myself by turning off my lights and sitting in my closet. I know this was probably a weird thing to do at my age, but I wanted seclusion. I wanted to hide. Christopher opened my door to find me there and I thoroughly freaked him out. I mean, I don't think he'll ever view me the same again. Christopher had oil and wanted to pray over me but I refused. My embarrassment was too great.

When we left for Calvary Church, I sat alone in the back, humiliated and ashamed. I may have ruined everything for the other guys, and I wasn't about to face their disap-

pointment in me. A new guy spoke tonight. Surprisingly, he wasn't half bad, and I was impressed with what he had to say.

Learning we were not going to be allowed to go to the beach made me feel incredibly guilty. Since Christopher canceled the beach trip after I confessed how difficult of a time I was having, I assumed the reason we weren't allowed to go was because of something I had done or said. At the time, it also seemed like Christopher did not want me to go to the beach and become tempted by seeing other men with their shirts off, the old Christian approach of reducing temptation by limiting access. Christopher may have seemed upset or freaked out by my revelations because he did not know how to deal with someone like me. The staff was mostly accustomed to treating substance users—not someone who was seeking to change their sexual orientation (who also happened to abuse substances). I suspect Christopher realized my situation was out of his league which is why he called in his wife Katherine to speak to me later that evening and canceled the beach trip.

DAY 9

The week before I left the Midwest for California, I had a sobering conversation with my parents and brother. The conversation was difficult because we laid everything out on the table. During our talk, my parents had me write down all my problematic characteristics. I appropriately labeled the sheet "Pandora's Box of Problems." The list included the following points:

I am not okay with myself
I deflect
I want validation from others
I justify my actions
I rely on others for acceptance
Nothing is my fault
I manipulate to get what I want
People pleaser
I refuse to take responsibility
Attempt to pull the wool over the eyes of others
I try to make people feel sorry for me
Obsess on myself
Don't feel okay in my own skin
Need to know root of behavior
Compare self to others
Lack pattern/routine
Unsure of self
Say sorry a lot

Don't feel worthy
Unable to receive love
Believe in lies
Dwell in self-pity
Feel like a 'problem' child
Blow up easily
Overly emotional
Take things to too seriously
I am sensitive
I have distorted filters
I twist things
I am judgmental
I have hate for my dad
I wear people out (use/abuse)
I tend to be negative
I run with bad people
I look for excuses
I am not light-hearted
I want to run away
I have an addictive personality
I am lonely

*This accurately describes where I feel I am and what needs
to change in addition to homosexual attraction. I don't
know how I can become a different person and how these
things can change, but maybe with God's help I can.*

I SHOULD COMMENT ON the "Pandora's Box of Problems" list. Reading
this list of "problems" ten years after the fact is difficult because it is
obvious I felt riddled with so much shame and guilt. Looking at this list is
terrifying and disturbing. I cannot imagine what any parent might think
if they found such a list created by one of their children. Truly. Many of
the items on the list can be said of most people, however, not just me.

These are common attributes of people who are insecure or unsure of themselves. However, because of my hyper-critical spirit and nature, I took everything about myself very seriously. When I showed my parents this list of problems, they agreed that these were true attributes of me at the time.

We had a meeting tonight with Jackie and she has an interesting way of addressing our past hurts. She pinpoints a prior painful or hurtful experience with a client, and asks them to visualize the specific time, place, and people present. She investigates the associated emotions from the memory, then examines the gravity of it all. When the individual settles into the memory, she asks the individual to picture Jesus in that memory. If the Lord is then willing, the individual experiences Jesus's security and love. The cycle of bondage is broken, and the individual is released from the past pain.

I was watching how she handled Marvin's memories. When asked to identify a painful experience, Marvin could not recall any. At the time, everyone's eyes were closed. I kept my eyes open, however, and gave Jackie a quizzical look. Hunter also had his eyes open and was looking at me. This was typical Hunter behavior, so I didn't think anything of it.

Since Marvin couldn't picture a specific time, Jackie asked him to describe his house growing up and went from there. She was able to identify the pain Marvin had received from his dad who refused to attend his little league ball games as a kid. Jackie encouraged Marvin to pick a specific incident, and Marvin said he had one in mind. Jackie encouraged him to picture Jesus, but he was unable to see Him. It seemed Jackie's method was not working on Marvin. I again opened my eyes and Hunter was still looking at me. I made eye contact, but Hunter's stare did not waver. I was still curious about what Jackie would do next with Marvin. Knowing

Marvin had a son, Jackie had him speak what Jesus could have said to Marvin's childhood self, which I thought was an interesting approach. She then had both Marvin's childhood-self and adult-self accept Jesus into their hearts, which she hoped would cause Jesus to appear. After the prayer, Marvin was again prompted to visualize Jesus. Marvin said Jesus had appeared. He was holding and touching his shoulder but was not saying anything. However, Marvin did state that he could feel Jesus loved him.

I got a little teary when Marvin identified the pain he felt from his father as I feel my own dad does not meet my emotional needs. Jackie noticed my tears, and asked what I was feeling. I expressed how I had anger towards my dad, God, and myself.

Jackie began to discuss how the father/son relationship tends to be something the devil manipulates. As Jackie said this, Hunter suddenly doubled over as if in pain, startling everyone present.

As Hunter fell to the floor, he began shaking as if experiencing a seizure. Weirdly, my immediate instinct was to put my hands out and begin speaking in tongues. Hunter was displaying symptoms of demonic possession. The shaking was out of control. His arms were crossed, and his hands were contorted. Hunter began making noises. Not actual words, but more like moaning, deep and unintelligible. Jackie and Katherine were on the ground, holding him and praying the blood of Jesus over him. This went on for a while. When his shaking and moaning subsided, Jackie and Katherine tried to lift him up. I was right in front of him. His face was contorted. His tongue was sticking out of his mouth. Hunter's breathing changed again, and the deep voice returned. He fell back onto the ground. A few moments later, while Katherine held his hand, Hunter gave a forced smile and uttered something like, "He wants us to praise

Him."

Jesus or Satan? Hunter did not or could not identify who "he" was. A few moments passed, and we all helped get Hunter in a chair as he began to recover. Katherine and Jackie went to the office to call 911. I sat next to Hunter, and he was able to open his eyes. However, just as he opened them, his eyes rolled back, and he began shaking again. His arms crossed, and the fingers of his right hand were all contorted. After calling 911, Jackie and Katherine came out and guided him into the office. They closed the door and that was the end of the session.

The paramedics showed up and Hunter immediately returned to normal. He was sent to the hospital for observation. I pray that he will be okay. I also pray that tonight results in a breakthrough for him. If there was a demonic influence, I hope it is now removed.

The rest of the guys and I were unsure what to do during this whole episode (or after), but we focused on prayer. We went outside to process.

Up until my time at NH, I had not yet experienced a grand mal seizure (except for at age six when I came out of my coma). Soon after I completed my time at NH in 2012, however, I experienced a seizure in 2013. The criterion for epilepsy is having two or more seizures. Therefore, after 2013, I was given the diagnosis of epilepsy. Epilepsy would become a struggle for me as I frequently began experiencing seizures and auras (precursors to full blown seizures). These were triggered by lack of sleep and stress, which are things I regularly dealt with.

Knowing what I now know, looking back on what happened with Hunter on day nine, I am baffled by the staff's initial response in praying the blood of Jesus over him instead of immediately calling 911. Due to the staff's over-spiritualization of everything they encountered, they assumed they were experiencing a spiritual event, rather than a medical one. It truly seems naive, irresponsible, and incompetent. If I had been the one having a seizure and the staff had merely prayed the blood of Jesus over me, I am genuinely curious what my parents would have done.

DAY 10

Christopher went into each room and had a five-to-ten-minute talk. I later discovered he was sharing who would be going on the beach trip and who wouldn't. Christopher did not come to my room. Instead, after talking with everyone else, he peeked in my room and asked if he and I were good. I said yes, hoping to avoid further drama. He said something like "I'm happy you dealt with the Holy Spirit." Really? I knew things would be awkward, but that was out of line. Whatever. That confirmed: I am never sharing with him again.

<hr/>

CHRISTOPHER'S QUESTION OF, "ARE we good?" was a bit ambiguous given that he could have been talking about multiple incidents: an incident with Hunter going to the hospital, forcing me to come out at a Christian AA meeting, or not informing me whether I would be going to the beach were all viable possibilities. The fact he only asked, "Are we good?" after having lengthy conversations with everyone else in the facility rubbed me wrong. Sure, I did not want to speak to him and yes, I did want to avoid drama. However, transparency would have been nice.

Although the staff left me in the dark regarding the beach trip and its primary purpose, I later learned why residents went to the beach.

Before Christopher left, he mentioned only a few guys will be going to the beach this weekend –those who need to work on their fourth step. Since I haven't even started the first step, I highly doubt I will be going.

The beach trip was specifically for individuals who were working through the steps of AA—specifically the fourth step (during which people take inventory of negative character traits). The time at Pismo Beach was a retreat to experience beauty and solitude, assisting those working through the fourth step. Given the lack of clarity regarding the purpose of the beach trip, I suspected I was being left out because I was gay. Although no one had said so, I assumed that the reason I was not invited was because they thought I would be tempted by seeing men without their shirts on. Their lack of transparency truly felt irresponsible and unfair.

DAY 11

Before going to bed last night, I created a list of sins I believe I need to repent from. I kept repeating 1 John 1:9 and got on my knees before the Lord. I didn't play games or pray intellectually. Instead, I got real about my sin. I started going down the list but didn't get all the way through it. I addressed hatred and disappointment toward my dad, the vast array of homosexual sins I have committed (hook-ups, thoughts, pornography, masturbation, messing around with multiple partners), my relationship with George (all the sin that came with it), and the anger/resentment I still hold toward high school classmates. I didn't make excuses but took ownership of my actions. I admitted my pride and lack of faith. I asked for help and forgiveness. I admitted I don't know the way and my heart is not in the right place.

FULLY SURRENDERING TO GOD is a phrase frequently used in Christian circles. This is in large part due to scripture. Romans 12:1 says:

"I appeal to you therefore, brothers, by the mercies of God, to present your bodies as a living sacrifice, holy and acceptable to God, which is your spiritual worship."[1]

Since no one can read or know another person's heart, or even their intentions, what does complete surrender look like? What is the practical twenty-first century version of a living sacrifice? Depending on your faith, this may mean different things to different people. Gavin's assertion that I had not fully surrendered my life to Christ made me feel gaslit. Here I was, a social worker who had committed to multiple levels of intervention from The Church to "save me." I had followed the rules, prayed the prayers, and read the scriptures. I served a year at a mega-church, accepted the leadership and discipleship of Campus Crusade, and sought out books and conferences to try to fix my own sexual orientation. This was all prior to entering NH. To suggest I was not a Christian and had not fully surrendered was out of line. I truly felt judged and wondered what Gavin would do if he were in my shoes.The Experiencing God class was challenging. I expressed some of my disagreements with the material. This resulted in some intriguing conversations. Gavin is so black and white in his views. I admit it's actually kind of entertaining challenging him. Experience has taught me that viewing things in black and white serves as a great security blanket, but it fails to truly encompass life's complexity. I challenged Gavin by saying while we must trust in Christ, we are still allowed to ask God questions. Gavin disagreed. His stance is "God knows what we need more than we do, and faith is trusting God and believing He knows best." I partly agree with his assertion, but I feel a relationship with God involves asking questions about my future. No agreement with Gavin was reached today, but this conversation branched into something interesting.

To my great discomfort, Gavin ran my logic into the ground. We discussed how our friendships and relationships must change to truly follow God. This conversation, while not heated, threw me overboard. My relationship history is far from positive. Heck, I don't think I've even had a true friend with the exception of my ex-girlfriend Jennifer and my friend Knives. Gavin made a definitive statement: "one thing has to change: everything." I ended up sharing my fear and doubt that true change is possible. Apparently, this triggered Gavin. He began a verbal tirade, saying for God to work we must fully turn from our sin. I shared I had fully turned from my sin. Oops, I shouldn't have said that.

Gavin looked me straight in the face, in-group nonetheless, and told me I am arrogant, prideful, and need to get over myself. He continued by saying he doesn't believe I am a Christian, and that I've never fully surrendered. I have not made efforts to change. He was direct. Forceful. He spoke as if all this was pure fact. I felt like I was a student or child who was being scolded. It was humiliating. At this point, I shut up.

Alex then started laughing and shared how he had been the same way. He talked about being stuck in cycles of self-pity and said how foolish he had been. I felt as if everyone was laughing at me.

Before ending our meeting, Gavin confronted me again. He asked what I was thinking. I stated I felt he was out of line, that he doesn't know my past, he doesn't know my heart, and he doesn't know how my relationship with Christ operates. Gavin claimed his summation was the only possible explanation because "God is faithful and just" and that is an absolute. He stated my fruits don't resemble those of someone who knows the Lord. When I humbly disagreed, he stated, "Well. Don't worry. You are going to be here a long time, so you'll figure it out." Words fail to express how I felt at that moment.

I learned a valuable lesson. Gavin is not someone I can trust, at least not in the presence of others. Gavin called me into his office. I was not okay with how he's treated me in-group, so I expected him to either apologize or further interrogate me. Instead, he ran through my treatment plan. I kept my mouth shut because I knew whatever I said could be used against me. I was surprised the treatment plan did not include anything pertaining to homosexuality. Instead, the objectives centered on negative thinking, alcohol/cannabis dependence, and knowledge of the Bible/relationship with Jesus, and relationships with others. The treatment plan was pretty standard, but I feel it fails in addressing my real reason for being here. At the end Gavin asked if I had anything on my mind. I did, but I refused to say anything. Gavin has proven he can't be trusted.

My interactions with Gavin recall a video by Andy Stanley. Andy Stanley is an evangelical pastor, the bestselling author of over twenty books, and a motivational speaker. If only Gavin could have Andy Stanley's perspective. In a sermon at Northpoint Church in Atlanta, Stanley said,

"...If we could get straight people as excited about serving and engaged as the gay men and women I know, we would have a volunteer backlog. That's my experience in our churches. A gay person who still wants to attend church, after the way The Church has treated the gay community. I'm telling you, they have more faith than I do. They have more faith than a lot of you. A gay person, who says, "You know what? I'm not going to be accepted here, but I'm going to try anyway..." Have you ever done that as a straight person? Where do you go that you're not sure you're going to be accepted? And you go over, and over, and over? Only your in-law's house. That's the only place you go where you know

you're not going to be completely accepted. Any place you go over and over and it's because you have to. But otherwise, what environment do you continue to step foot in, knowing that any moment you may feel ostracized? I'm telling you, the gay men and women who grew up in church, and the gay men and women who come to Christ as adults, who want to participate in our church? Oh, my goodness. I know 1 Corinthians 6, and I know Leviticus, and I know Romans. It's so interesting to talk about all that stuff...The gay man or woman who wants to worship their heavenly father, who did not answer the cry of their heart when they were twelve, or thirteen, or fourteen, and fifteen? God said "no". And they still love God? We have some things to learn from a group of men and women."

Later that day, I wrote in my journal:

I called home after our group. I had Mom check my student email but there wasn't anything significant. I also had her check my Facebook. I only had 6 notifications and two emails. I was disappointed. George sent me an email on Facebook. Jackpot. This is what I wanted to see! He sent me a dramatic and emotional song with Georgish lyrics. No surprise. It was nice to see my absence hasn't gone unnoticed. The lyrics gave me enough insight to know George is supporting my treatment and isn't sitting around hating me.

My mom said she is praying for me and that I should change my focus. She expressed that she doesn't think I'm a Christian. Developing a relationship with Christ should be where I spend my time and focus on my treatment, not becoming straight. Interesting. Is this a sign from God or has NH been talking with my parents? I requested to have my dad text Katherine and get Davis, my friend, okayed to come see me.

The course this conversation with my mother took was not that surprising. While I went to NH focused on becoming straight, my sexuality had not been my parents' only concern. They were concerned about how out of control my life had become, my sexuality was only a part of it. My mother did not want me to lose sight of the bigger picture. I had been using substances as a way of coping with an evangelical worldview, experiencing the devastation from realizing I was gay. My mother stating that I was not a Christian was over the top and, quite honestly, hurtful. I now understand she was responding to my resistance to the program. She viewed my resistance as insubordination, failing to understand that I was truly struggling with the premise of changing my sexuality. I could not see beyond that aim to benefit from the other aspects of my treatment.

DAY 12

Jackie came to meet with me. We talked for four hours! So much was said, I wish I could have recorded it so I could remember everything. One thing was for certain: the Holy Spirit was present, and I was honest.

*Jackie has a theory that I have developed a religious spirit. While I know **about** God and know scripture, I do not **know** God and am deceived. I can "talk the talk" but I can't "walk the walk." This is because I have been in control—my "self" is still on the throne, but I am able to camouflage myself with knowledge and words about God, good works, and my intelligence. I dress the part but deep down I am a fraud.*

Jackie explored my need for control with me, and came to the conclusion that at a very, very young age I felt I couldn't be myself. I became protective of my mom and strived to please her. A very young version of myself is trapped inside of me. I display a false self and use religion for protection, keeping people away, staying in control. In order for me to be freed from this control, I must surrender, let go, and fall into the arms of Christ's love. Sounds easy, right? Jackie tried to take me back to being my younger self, but I couldn't do it. Letting go requires blind faith, like jumping off a cliff and trusting someone will be there to catch me, which is terrifying to me. Jackie said that until I am willing to fully surrender, let go of control, and trust God to catch me, I will not get better. I will always have trust issues, feel distant from God, and live life in bondage. She encouraged me to take on extreme faith, being broken. If I mentally can't do it, I need to try and physically do it. I must reach a point where the only thing able to save me is Christ. I knew she was right, but the truth hurt.

WITH TWO OF THE guys from the program at the beach, I can remember day twelve feeling both awkward and special at the same time. I had formed a meaningful friendship with Alex and relied on him for stability through the beginning of this experience. With his absence came a sense of loneliness. Alex and Kevin's absence, however, meant the staff was more focused on me—my problems and the real reason I came to this program in the first place. Being able to spend four hours with Jackie, for example, would never have been possible with everyone else present at the facility.

Katherine came to see me. I get really nervous meeting with her because I really don't want to look bad in front of her. She is the boss and I'm scared she will see past my false self and see the facade of who I am. The meeting went okay. She addressed a few of my issues such as pride, rebelliousness, and negative thinking. She stated I must capture, submit, replace and repent of my problems and these types of desires when they arise. I find this very difficult and verbalized some resistance.

Day twelve had heavy hitting punches. Most notably, the staff wanted me to understand that my pride was a significant problem and only true surrender would result in the change I was seeking. Katherine, Jackie, and Gavin all came at me with different approaches but a similar message:

I needed to surrender. Katherine's message of "capture, submit, replace and repent" sounded like the Apostle Paul's message in 2 Corinthians 10:5 where he notes:

> *"We destroy arguments and every lofty opinion raised against the knowledge of God, and take every thought captive to obey Christ."*[1]

The message? I needed to take my thoughts captive (capture), understand (submit) and replace them with holy thoughts (replace), and seek God's forgiveness for such actions (repent). However, I still wonder - is this what true surrender looks like? Even in the program the concept of "surrender" was vague and ambiguous. There did not appear to be any specific roadmap other than the general "capture, submit, replace, and repent," which solely deals with one's thoughts and not their actions (much less their sexual attractions).

It was hard not to feel judgmental toward the staff. At the time, I honestly felt I could have run the program better (which I realize is kind of arrogant to say). The very behaviors the staff were trying to instill within me did not seem like characteristics and behaviors they themselves possessed. Gavin and Christopher were perfect examples of this discrepancy. Gavin came across as extremely judgmental, and I always felt guarded around him. Christopher felt like a loose cannon, ready to blow off at any given moment. There were things about him I looked up to, and I felt I could trust him most of the time. But there were instances, such as when he forced me out of the closet at an AA meeting, which made me have utter distaste for him.

DAY 13

I've refused to 'submit' to God. I've been unable to allow God to work in my life. In order to be used by God or to even experience God, I must relinquish control. It's almost humorous how unwilling I have been to do that. I've been blinded by my pride and my control, but God has been revealing my need for Him. I'm scared of losing the little control I do have but am excited God is working. I've never truly trusted God or anyone.

God has been revealing how pathetic I've been in handling my homosexuality. I've used my struggle as justification for rebellion and sin, which is foolish. The solution is not for God to 'heal' me or for Him to take the struggle away. The solution resides in humbling myself to God and submitting to his will. Homosexuality is not something I can use against God. It is a symptom of a lack of faith, and the selfish desire I possess to fulfill instant gratification. It essentially comes down to me being in 'control.' I don't need anti-gay therapy. I need Godliness and humility.

The extent of my selfishness and pride is becoming more apparent. For years, I've used my biblical knowledge and theology to make myself feel better and justify my actions. I have created my plans and set my path—doing what I've wanted and asking God to bless my choices. All the while,

I had never fully surrendered to God, and sought my own will! No wonder my life has turned out the way it has.

———◦———

I HAVE REMARKED ON this in prior days, but if you haven't already, you will notice a continual day-to-day pendulum swing in my thinking at NH. One moment I'd say the program was helping, then in the same entry would say the program was detrimental, the next day saying I wanted to grow close to God, but then wanting to throw in the towel, wanting to change my sexuality, to desiring to stay gay. This back-and-forth continues going forward in my journal. Part of what drove this divided mindset was my state of constant fear and denial—denial of my substance use, fear of my own realization about my sexuality. I do not think, however, that I have said anything inaccurate, inappropriate, disrespectful, or wrong regarding the staff at NH.

DAY 14

I used my cell to call my dad and it turns out, I also had a text message from Justin. Justin left a voicemail telling me that he was hanging out with Knives at a rock show. He shared that both of them have been praying for me and miss me greatly. It was so nice to hear that they're hanging out. They love the Lord and are living for Him, not to mention they care about me.

SINCE THIS WAS A relaxed day with others at the beach, I had the opportunity to call my parents. In speaking with them, I remember sharing my concerns with my dad. Points I recall include the following:

1) I realized how my pride, arrogance, and lack of a real relationship with Christ led to all my problems. I had learned how to change that but staying at the program was only going to postpone dealing with it.

2) Fundamentalism was the prevalent perspective of the staff, and having fundamentalism constantly pushed on me would only lead me back into my judgmental past.

3) I met with Jackie and Katherine once a week. That was good, but the rest of the time, I was not really learning or gaining anything beneficial.

4) Gavin was extremely judgmental and, as a result, I found it hard to take him seriously.

5) I was away from the outside world. I needed to feel connected to the real world to seal my plans.

6) While I was there, I was losing valuable career experience.

7) I was not happy. I was in complete agreement that I should be receiving help. For example, I believed I should be meeting with a professional psychologist or a counselor. I could have also been working and reconciling my relationships with my Christian friends. Instead, I was in California (getting what I needed once a week) and suffering the rest of the time.

I remember my dad listened and agreed with me. He agreed to start seeking alternative professional help for me and would call Katherine sometime later. Meanwhile, he told me to do my best—talk and share my concerns with Katherine and finish out the month. At this point in the journey, I fully believed that if all went according to plan, I would leave in two weeks. I can remember this provided a sense that there was a light at the end of the tunnel.

DAY 15

I am realizing my relationships have suffered due to control issues stemming from my 'false self.' I've developed a list of problems (those listed in the January 9 entry). Relationships haven't worked because I have been in denial, and I have been in search of validation. The answer is not becoming straight but accepting myself as a homosexual. If I continue to try to change my sexual preference, I will only continue to live in denial and my 'false self' will only become more defined. I need to learn what the Lord has spoken to me instead of relying on what others tell me. I must, and will, be held accountable for what the Lord has told me—not what other well-meaning Christians have told me. I am accountable to God, not man. What should I do now?

I know this realization will never fly with the staff. I am guessing they will try to convince me I am wrong (because six verses in the Bible say so). I am worried that if I share all of this with them, I will be told I need to stay here longer. They will try and do everything to break me and convince me that what the Lord shared with me is false. I don't know what to do!

Before we left for church today, I prayed that God would confirm what He shared with me last night. We went to church at The Gate. During worship, they sang a song with the lyrics "I love you just as you are." At that moment, my

45

answer was received, and His revelation was confirmed. The problem has not been that I'm gay, the problem has been my trying to change. God loves me and his heart is broken since I have hated myself for my same-sex attraction. It feels too good to be true. I'm struggling to believe this because I haven't believed it since I was a little boy. The great thing is, God is bigger than people and He is bigger than my understanding.

READING THIS ENTRY TEN years later makes for an interesting experience. I feel this entry would have made for a great ending to my coming out story. However, this was only day fifteen. There were more than seventy days to come and more internal conflict to work through. Having said that, I am unsure of what led me to feel less sinful at this point in the journey other than mere exasperation, fear, and a desire for answers. I recall coming before the Lord, lying prostrate in my room, scared and crying, unsure of what would happen next. At the same time, however, a sense of peace and tranquility fell upon me, provided through prayer. It was this peace and tranquility that led me to believe God loved me no matter what. Gavin's more judgmental diatribes also motivated this new viewpoint. I have never been one to easily receive rejection and that was what I felt in this program. Gavin was rebuking me, saying I was a wolf in sheep's clothing and a fraud. To have the staff making assumptions about me, while I was seeking treatment to change, felt like a betrayal. The opposite of betrayal is acceptance. I held on to the need for acceptance, prayed for acceptance, craved it, and sought after this until eventually I believed it. *Day Fifteen was a significant turning point in the story of my stay at NH.*

I may have made a grave mistake. I called home and shared these recent thoughts with my dad. I was one hundred percent transparent with him, saying I think I can be proud of being gay. He was clearly very upset, but this is between the Lord and me: I can't be responsible for him. He really doesn't get it, but he promised me that he wouldn't torture me by making me stay here. All I must do is last the next two weeks. I pray God is faithful and will see to it that my dad keeps his word. Now... to redo my homework, read my Bible, and then go to bed.

On Day Fifteen, I called my father to inform him of my newfound revelation from God: that I was okay with being gay, and God accepted and loved me regardless. My father agreed with the premise that God loved me but did not agree that God had made me gay. My father was spending a ton of money to not only get me sober, but also help me find a resolution to my sexuality. Therefore, my giving up fifteen days into the program likely seemed a bit hasty and unrealistic to him. My father's only compromise was for me to stay an additional two weeks and re-evaluate at the end of that time. My dad did provide me with a sense of hope by saying I was not going to be stuck in this program forever, that finding acceptance could be a way forward.

DAY 16

I know Matthew read my journal this morning. In morning meditation, he taught, "You cannot live contrary to the Word of God and be in the will of God." True, but what about 'gay theology'? Katherine's book addresses 'gay theology' but fails to adequately dismiss it. The six verses in the Bible can be reasoned away. There is no definitive condemnation of homosexuality in Scripture. It actually requires faith to believe in this condemnation. This, in combination with what the Lord shared with me, did not convict me to change. Instead, it led me to believe it's okay to be gay. I feel peace with my sexuality. I truly do. I just need to keep my mouth shut and not share any of this in groups. I hope and pray the Lord still uses today's groups to speak to me.

AS A CLIENT, I had to keep a journal. I had brought my own and was keeping that one to myself, but I turned my treatment journal in every evening. Staff read over journals each night to ensure the following:

1) We were indeed journaling.

2) We were applying concepts learned in the program into our lives.

3) Follow-up on anything that had us upset or confused.

Since the staff were regularly reading my journal, I viewed my entries as a way of surreptitiously communicating with the staff. It was my opportunity to speak with the staff about my feelings and thoughts without their input and critiques. It therefore did not surprise me when Matthew started the day with a study focused on the common evangelical adage, *"You cannot live contrary to the Word of God and be in the will of God."*

> *While the affirmation of 'gay theology' is frowned upon here, I find its arguments not only convincing but also somewhat compelling. Here are the six "clobber verses" against homosexuality, and gay theology's arguments against them:*
>
> *First Verse: "But before they lay down, the men of the city, the men of Sodom, both young and old, all the people to the last man, surrounded the house. And they called to Lot, 'Where are the men who came to you tonight? Bring them out to us, so that we may know them.' Lot went out to the men at the entrance, shut the door after him and said, 'I beg you, my brothers, do not act so wickedly.'" — Genesis 19:4-7*
>
> *Objections: The Bible does not say these men were homosexual. In some translations of the Bible, scripture is cross referenced which refers to this passage being the sin of a 'lack of hospitality' in Ezekiel 16:49 which reads "Behold, this was the guilt of your sister Sodom: she and her daughters had pride, excess of food and prosperous ease, but did not aid the poor and needy." There is no Biblical statement indicating homosexual intent on the part of the townspeople.*

Second Verse: "You shall not lie with a male as with a woman; it is an abomination." — Leviticus 18:22

AND

Third Verse: "If a man lies with a male as with a woman, both of them have committed an abomination; they shall surely be put to death; their blood is upon them." — Leviticus 20:13

Objections: *Both Scriptures are sandwiched between other prohibitions that we no longer hold valid—are we to pick and choose which of the Old Testament commandments we follow? If some commandments are obsolete, then why consider the commandments condemning homosexuality as valid?*

Fourth Verse: "For this reason God gave them up to dishonorable passions. For their women exchanged natural relations for those that are contrary to nature; and the men likewise gave up natural relations with women and were consumed with passion for one another, men committing shameless acts with men and receiving in themselves the due penalty for their error." — Romans 1:26-27

Objections: *What is natural? The phrase: 'against nature' translates to para physin in the Greek which means "against 'origin, source (closely connected with) creation and meaning the natural condition, or the regular order of things.'" Gay theology argues that individuals are 'born gay' and are therefore following their 'natural' inclinations by engaging in homosexual acts, they are not acting against their nature. Thus, this verse does not apply to individuals who are born gay. However, it could apply to individuals who are heterosexual but decide to participate in homosexual acts.*

Fifth Verse: "Or do you not know that the unrighteous

will not inherit the kingdom of God? Do not be deceived: neither the sexually immoral, nor idolaters, nor adulterers, nor men who practice homosexuality, nor drunkards, nor revilers, nor swindlers will inherit the kingdom of God. And such were some of you. But you were washed, you were sanctified, you were justified in the name of the Lord Jesus Christ and by the Spirit of our God." — 1 Corinthians 6:9-11

Objections: *This is the only passage in the entire Bible that states that homosexuality can be changed and it's in a long list of other sins!*

Sixth Verse: The Creation Story (Citing that Adam and Eve were created male and female—that God intended males and females to only be attracted to the opposite gender when He created them.)

Objections: *I find no need to reference this passage, as most are fully aware of the Adam and Eve story found in Genesis. My objection to it is that the Creation Story has nothing to do with homosexuality.*

Considering the analysis on gay theology, I still believe in the premise of and foundation behind the critical evaluation of scripture. For years, I took the Bible at face value, trying to apply it to my life without considering that I was reading a translation, someone's interpretation of the text from a different language. Bias is clearly there. Therefore, I must earnestly critique these scriptures. After careful thought and study, I have concluded there *is not* sufficient evidence to support the claim that:

1) Homosexuality is a sin and

2) God is adamantly against it.

In fact, I would go as far as to reason that homosexuality could be God's answer to overpopulation in the world, but I digress. I very much support claims and arguments that critically analyze the hermeneutical context of the six verses used to condemn being gay within the context of the Bible.

I just had my meeting with Jackie. After talking, I agreed to let go of my control and allowed myself to re-experience painful childhood memories. I first went back to elementary school, to Mr. C's classroom. Everyone was laughing, but I felt nervous and scared. I felt alienated and alone. I was jealous of the friendships all the other kids seemed to have, and I felt I could not be a part of it because I was different, and there was something wrong with me.

The Lord took me back to our extended family's cabin. I was in the yard with my friends Billy and Jeremy. We were doing backflips on an inflated tube near a tree. I couldn't recall what was said, but I felt excluded. I wanted to fit in and be a part of the group, but I wasn't. I became upset and yelled, "Shut up, you idiot!" This is still a common joke with Billy and Jeremy today. As I was exploring the alienation I felt from this event, my mom's voice entered my mind. "Why can't you be as athletic as Jeremy?" "Why are you so serious?" "Why can't you be as light-hearted as Billy?"

The Lord took me back to being a little kid in the downstairs bedroom. I was sitting on the bed and my mom was standing in the doorway. She asked me questions about school and asked me why I wasn't like everyone else. All my feelings of inadequacy came rushing back.

Jackie asked me to picture Jesus. Was he in the room? Out of nowhere, an individual appeared on bended knee in front of me. He looked me in the eye and extended out his hand. With a quiet, yet powerful voice, he spoke over my mom. "You are not inadequate. I made you just as you are.

You don't need to be like anyone else." Upon hearing these words, I began to cry. I was a young boy, I don't know how old. Jackie asked me to reach out and hold his hand, but I couldn't. The room became dark and cold.

Jackie must have noticed my change in demeanor and asked me what was wrong. I whispered, "He's in the room." Thankfully, she understood what I meant and asked the Lord to reveal where the devil was. I freaked out and became extremely scared. There I was, a little boy sitting on the bed. Jesus was on bended knee in front of me, but behind me was a dark figure. He was on the bed with both hands covering my eyes and my mouth. The dark figure was massive and stood two or three feet taller than me. He wasn't clear but he was large and had a black appearance.

Jackie told me to ask Jesus for protection, but at first nothing happened. Satan had a hold of me. I waited thirty seconds and the Jesus figure got brighter. I was scared because the dark figure seemed to be bigger than Jesus. Then all of a sudden, Jesus moved faster than I could see towards Satan and Satan disappeared into one of the corners of the room. With a flash of an eye, Jesus was back in front of me with his arm outstretched.

Jackie prompted me to ask how Satan was able to enter into my life. Jesus looked me in the eye. He said, "It's because I've chosen you. I want to use you." Jackie asked me what he said but I hesitated. I told her that I feared it was arrogant. She asked me to tell her anyway, so I did. She then said it was the real Jesus, and I wasn't being arrogant. I grabbed the hand of Jesus and squeezed. A tear fell from his eye and at that point, I was fully aware that Jesus loved me.

With Jackie's leading, I cast out all demonic presences in my life and proclaimed the blood of Jesus over me. I surrendered myself under the authority of Christ. I agreed to not just believe but to walk with Him.

Jackie led me in a prayer in forgiving my mom. Mom wasn't aware of what was going on. Satan had used her without her knowing. I forgave her. Then, Jackie told me I had to break free from my mom's control and expectations. I now fully belong to Christ and not to her. I walked up, gave her a hug and closed the door.

It was just Jesus and I in the room now. I asked Christ if there was anyone else who I should forgive. I asked if I should forgive my dad and Christ said, "Yes but not now." I asked if there was anyone else. He looked me in the eye and said, "You need to forgive yourself." As the little boy, I began to cry, and Christ took me into his arms. Jackie led me into a prayer of forgiveness.

Jesus told me I didn't need to ask for forgiveness for anyone else at this time. I said goodbye and he gave me a big hug. He whispered into my ear, "It's going to be okay. I am in control, and I have a plan for your life. Have faith."

I looked up at Jackie with tears in my eyes. I had just met Jesus. I realize there has been a demonic presence in my life since I was a little boy. Jesus sent the demon away and told me that because He called me and gave me a specific task for Him, Satan wanted to do anything and everything to prevent it. I have now surrendered my life to Christ fully and agreed to walk under His authority, which is His Word.

Jackie explained how walking in the Spirit requires total submission. It's not about who I am (whether that person is gay or straight) but rather about who Christ is. I have been trying to fit God into my life and for him to approve of my gay identity. All the while, this is not the way this works. It isn't about who I'm attracted to, it's about what Christ wants. I'm now under His authority, not my own. If

Christ provides someone for me to be with, so be it. (It will most likely not be a male). That isn't the point. The point is submission to God. Not my will but Christ's will be done!

I remember this day as being quite traumatic. Jackie's intervention did have actual therapeutic aspects to it. Mental health professionals often employ these types of practices; however, they do not use a "spiritual approach." Mixing real psychology with religion complicates things. The emotions and memories brought up in Day Sixteen's session were real. However, Jackie forced me to contrive the spiritual aspects. I remember producing the story of the demon holding his hands over my eyes and mouth to exemplify how trapped I felt. I do not feel this was a genuine interaction with a spiritual being but rather my own process of explaining my situation.

Since I experienced a "supposed" demonic presence, I should be honest about what I now feel. I do not have an answer. What I do know is this: I have had experiences in my life that I cannot explain. One could argue the spirit world had influenced these experiences. However, I do believe that people can (and often do) over-spiritualize weird or unusual occurrences, accrediting them to heaven and hell, good and bad, God and Satan. The question of the existence of a spirit world is an age-old puzzle, and one I do not want to try to solve here. Therefore, ten years later, I am extremely cautious in crediting things to spiritual warfare, or to attribute specific events to a spiritual being, whether that be God or the Devil (*if* they exist). Rather, I hold fast to a quote by Aleksandr Solzhenitsyn which states,

"The line separating good and evil passes not through states, nor between classes, nor between political parties either—but right through every human heart—and through all human hearts."[1]

I believe we as humans have the power to do good or do evil, and I do not attribute such actions as influenced by a spiritual force. Having said that, is "The Devil" real? Heck if I know.

DAY 17

I can't get out of my head. I believe I accepted Christ into my life, and I live under his authority, but I'm still troubled. I truly believe I am gay—I really do. I like men, period. Does this mean I don't have a relationship with God? Half, if not more, Christians now accept homosexuality. So, who do I believe? I've placed my care under a sect of Christianity believing homosexuality is sinful, but who is to say they are right? Believing in something that goes against my very being doesn't sound like faith, it sounds like torture. The more time I spend here, the more I discover who I am and understand how I think. It is becoming more and more clear that I am gay. All the while, I am growing closer to Christ! It seems Christ isn't saying 'either/or' but rather 'both.' I hear God saying, "I love you just as you are" and "Live your life for me, I will work through you" and "Everything is going to be okay." I'm not hearing, "Come to me and I'll make you straight." I feel God telling me one thing while this facility is telling me something different. Who do I trust, this facility or God?

I just got off the phone with my mom and I'm burning with anger. I tried to explain my current frustrations, but she wouldn't have it. I asked her if I was coming home on the first of the month, and she said that wasn't up to me. She stated it's up to her, Dad, and Katherine. Nothing is in my control! She implied that I have a terrible attitude and it is apparent I'm not walking in the Spirit. My mom brought up words I had said before I left. I had shared that my life was unmanageable—I only had a few real friends. I was not happy and felt distant from God. My mom then proceeded to question why I was so hung up on homosexuality. She stressed that homosexuality is only one problem in a list of many. She said it shouldn't be my first priority. I began to argue but had to end the call to go to the Overcomer's Meeting. I was fuming.

I feel as though there is something wrong with me. Life isn't supposed to be this difficult. My problem is clear: I have a religious spirit. My heart is so hard it seems impenetrable, like it's under lock and key. I'm miserable and I feel I can't do anything about my life as I watch it fall apart. I see the Lord at work in other people. I watch others change, but it doesn't seem possible for me. I feel hopeless. All my old mental tapes are blaring across my conscience: "There is something wrong with you," "You're a failure," "You're too messed up to have friends," "There is no hope," "You're a fag," "God hates you," "You're letting your parents down," and "Just give up like you always do."

The staff repeatedly say, "Die to yourself," "Die to yourself." Well, what if I don't? What if I'm incapable of change? Then what? My life is a wreck and all I see are my failures. I'm afraid to speak my mind for fear of judgment. I can practically hear the guys thinking, "When is this kid going to get a grip and get it?" I'm a king at missing the point and I think I missed the biggest one: my life!

———◇———

IN THIS ENTRY, I mentioned that my mother questioned why I was so hung up on homosexuality. This was partly because her reasons for entering me into NH's program were multiple, not merely for changing my sexuality. There was a profound difference between how my parents and I viewed my reasons for treatment. The truth was my life *had* become unmanageable. This was partly due to my own poor choices with substance use. Alcohol and drugs were why my parents found a program that not only could provide gay conversion therapy but also specialized in substance use recovery. Looking back, I honestly do not know whether homosexuality or substance abuse was their primary concern. It may have been a combination of both. For myself, however, I viewed the primary concern to be my sexual orientation. I felt it was what was driving my discontent and resulting behaviors. If I could resolve my sexuality, I believed I would no longer need substances to manage the stress of feeling rejected by the Christian faith. Because I felt sexually confused, I could not find peace and acceptance within The Church—the old cliché of trying to fit a round peg into a square hole. It was out of relentless exasperation that I felt the need to ask to go into treatment in the first place.

DAY 18

I'm feeling an overwhelming sense of guilt. I don't know what I should be doing. My life has been so messed up and confusing. While I was in college, I had a mission and direction. I dealt with my life by going to class, studying, and doing Christian ministry events. In California I have nothing to look forward to. I have nothing to distract me or take my mind off all my problems. It's miserable and it's driving me insane. I wish I had a good book, something allowing me to engage my mind, and escape from my current situation, even if only for an hour.

I BROUGHT A BOOK to the facility. However, based on NH' rules, the staff had to approve any books. The staff determined "The Girl Who Played with Fire" was not "Christian" and they confiscated the book on the first day. The staff told me reading while in treatment was inappropriate. They did not want any outside influences impacting my treatment (including, but not limited to, secular authors).

I can't believe the arrogance and pride I've had. I have been acting in total contempt. It's embarrassing I thought that way! I was again tempted to lust after the worship leader. I swear the devil is at work. Instead of indulging in my flesh, though, I closed my eyes during worship and practiced the "capture. submit. replace. repent" method. It wasn't completely effective, but it did keep my mind centered on Christ. To my great surprise, something changed in my heart. Apparently, God honored my effort and submission because the Spirit started to convict me. With my eyes closed, I felt connected with God and got emotional. It was like a breath of fresh air.

The service was dedicated to communion, and they had a guest speaker. I took a few notes I thought were worthwhile. Some of the notes included the following: "Don't allow sin to dictate your life. We have power over sin, sin doesn't have to dominate us. God will bring sorrow and pain in order to lead us to repentance—He loves us so much, and it's time to clean house." Yes, I know these aren't life-changing or revolutionary thoughts, but the Spirit was at work within me, and the thoughts were encouraging.

The Holy Spirit wasn't done with me. On the way home, God began to reveal how foolish I have acted toward the staff at NH. I've been prideful, arrogant, somewhat disrespectful, and ungrateful. I have sought every excuse to reason away my sin and have refused to humble myself. I need to take a hard look at myself and re-examine my motives for being here. I'm here to get to know Christ and get help, not to defend what I believe or think is right. It's time to quit the games, get real with my sin, and fall in humble surrender before the cross.

When we got home, Matthew called me to the office and gave me a letter from my parents. I was expecting a long letter detailing how the Lord saved me in a car wreck and how the devil is after me due to the gifts God gave me – how much potential I have to be used by God. Instead, my dad had photocopied a letter I had written to them. Shocking.

Reading my own words of surrender and thankfulness, I cried as I read. My dad is so clever. The letter was the most powerful and humbling thing I could receive while I'm here.

Was I prideful and arrogant? I do not want to present myself as having been perfect because I was not. I was far from it, in fact. Because I had recently graduated with my Social Work degree, I felt I knew what should be done in a treatment facility (or at least what treatment should entail). I may have occasionally presented myself as prideful, given my resistance to how things were being done at NH. However, was this truly "pride"? Or was it an appropriate reaction given the way the staff were running the facility and treatment application? I will leave that judgment up to the reader.

DAY 19

After a ten-minute break, we returned to another group Bob led. He had us write down our four current life priorities. I had already been feeling the Holy Spirit at work within me. Even before this meeting, the Holy Spirit had been convicting and humbling me. I have been so incredibly selfish during my mere twenty-two years of life. The Holy Spirit made sure I was aware of it. Therefore, I decided to get real during this group.

READING ABOUT THE PRIORITIES I identified on this day is alarming. I no longer prioritize these former aspects of my life. In fact, reading these priorities paints a good picture of where I was at the time – what I found important, and where my head was. Therefore, I would like to process how I currently view each of the priorities and identify how these priorities have changed.

#1 Priority: my relationship with the Lord, learning to walk the walk and talk the talk. I explained how this is all-encompassing—the rest of my priorities can be summed up in this one. The rest of the group identified the Lord as their number one as well. No surprises there. I mean, as a

Christian, God should always be the top priority, and if He's not, there is a problem.

Priority #1 was centered on my relationship with the Lord, which obviously needed to be number one. I was in a religious substance-use facility that prioritized God above everything else. As noted, everyone else in the program also identified their relationship with God as number one. If I had not done so, I suspect there would have been further questions and doubts about my spirituality from the staff and my fellow residents.

#2 Priority: my relationships with others. I explained that my sexual addiction turned me into a selfish and pathetic individual. I would reach out to Christians and ask for their support. I did this as a mere formality, fulfilling some type of Godly obligation. Yet, it was just that: me acting out of obligation. I had no intention of actually changing my behavior or taking the steps necessary toward sexual purity. As a result, and as they rightly should have, my Christian brothers gave up on me. My Christian community evaporated and I found myself digging further and further into addiction and drifting farther and farther from God. Like me, my new friends lacked integrity, character, and most importantly, a relationship with God. Before boarding the flight to California, I could count the Christian friendships I still held on one hand. Thus, my number two priority is, if possible, to seek reconciliation with my old friends and to create new friends who embody integrity, character, and relationship with God.

Priority #2 focused on my relationships with others: how I was engaging with the Christian community. It was obvious I downplayed my relationship with Christ and relationship to the Christian community to justify why I was experiencing same-sex attraction. I was unnecessarily negative in this section as I was not fair to all the attempts that I had made at living life the way I had been told. Such statements as "I had no intention of actually changing my behavior or taking necessary steps to find sexual purity" simply were not true. I *had* tried my hardest to commit to the Lord's will and had gone out of my way to try to change my sexuality. This included doing things that resulted in blatant humiliation such as openly talking to people and seeking guidance through Campus Crusade. However, while in this program, I needed to put my efforts down to fall in line and explain why I was not "sufficient."

> *#3 Priority: die to myself: surrender. For all the time I've spent in The Church and in service to God, I never fully surrendered to Him. In fact, I did the opposite. Church has been an opportunity for me to feel good about myself. I used church to boost my self-esteem and to gain a positive reputation. Christ hasn't been my God, I have been my own god. I need to surrender. By that, I don't mean an emotional performance during a worship service. No, I mean actual surrender. I must die to myself. I've expressed my fear in doing this, but God has made it clear I can no longer let fear hold me back. I must die to myself! No more excuses: this is mandatory!*

Priority #3 was all about surrender, which had become a phrase incessantly used by the staff. Surrendering was a practice Jackie, Gavin, and others frequently told me I was not carrying out. However, there was no tangible "This is what surrender looks like." Rather, the concept of surrender was ambiguous terminology used to describe the transformation – transformation that supposedly took place in someone's life when Christ became center according to the staff's perspective. The key was this: *Surrender was only legitimatized through the staff's perspective.* The only evidence I could possibly give of my "true surrender" would have been jumping up and saying, "Wow! God has fixed me and I'm not gay anymore!" (which obviously would have been a lie). Otherwise, in their eyes, I wasn't surrendering hard enough. I had become so swayed by the staff's perspective, I felt the need to put myself down and discredit my relationship with Christ and the steps I had already taken.

#4 Priority: end my continual cycle of depravity. Before coming to NH, I spent almost three years in a continual cycle of depravity. I would go to Church, get my "Jesus-fix," only to dive headfirst into sexual encounters. Guilt and shame would set in, and I would medicate with alcohol and the occasional joint. For a while marijuana became routine. More guilt and shame would come barreling in from that, and I would return to my "Jesus-fix." After getting some Jesus, the cycle would continue. I've spent years stuck in this cycle, unsure of how to break it. Thus, it's a priority of mine to put an end to this perpetual brokenness.

Priority #4 focused on my so-called depravity. Quite frankly, depravity was a dramatic and extreme way to describe my Jesus-fix → hookup → alcohol/marijuana cycle. Looking at it ten years later, I would not consider these actions "depraved," but rather an unhealthy cycle fueled by my need for acceptance and love. As I previously stated, "I would go to Church, get my 'JESUS' fix and then dive headfirst into sexual encounters, both random and scheduled. The guilt and shame would set in, and I would medicate with alcohol and the occasional joint." I do not believe the roots of my problems resided in same-sex attraction itself but stemmed from a religious system that chose to use guilt and shame as the primary means to repentance, repentance leading to conformity (i.e., control) in what my religious system wanted me to be, and conformity the only method to gain acceptance and love within that system.

As I look back on these priorities, it really reveals the place my heart and soul were regarding self-acceptance. It is now evident I was allowing religion to define my own worth and value. Further, I allowed religion to control my sense of well-being and sense of self. This was driven by a deep sense of self-hatred.

DAY 20

We did "Experiencing God" by watching a video on a 'Love Relationship God.' It was okay, same old-same old. The discussion afterward was interesting. I intentionally didn't speak because I'm trying to let the Holy Spirit work. Without saying anything, I was brought into the conversation. Ian said that yesterday when I had mentioned my critical nature, he told himself "What an idiot." Okay, where did that come from? Then Hunter added that he could see my critical nature from the moment I walked in the front door from day one. What am I to make of this? Without even speaking, I felt like I was thrown under a bus. How did those comments even relate to the topic of the video? I'm torn between two emotions. I want to be angry, but then again, I feel this may be God at work again. I don't know what to think. I'm trying to be humble.

I went outside with Marvin and Alex and listened to them talk. I didn't talk. My knees were shaking like crazy. My anxiety was off the chain. I'm not sure what to make of what the Lord is doing. I followed Marvin and Alex back inside, and we began the movie "The Blind Side." This made me extremely happy: an opportunity to get out of my head!

I FOUND IT STRANGE that Ian called out me and Hunter without prompting. I was already feeling down on this day and really needed a break from the constant barrage of condemnation. Receiving this level of criticism intensified everything I was already feeling. Upon reflection, I still do not know what instigated the critical nature of their comments. I was trying to be quiet on this day and simply sit back to reflect. I remember feeling betrayed by Hunter, but not shocked by Ian's words. I was more irritated with him. However, it felt unexpected and an attack for which I was clearly not prepared.

> *Gavin came to work. For exercise time, he brought a Christian golf movie called "7 Days in Utopia." I actually really like it and I know my dad would love it. However, the main actor is the same guy who starred in "Brokeback Mountain" with Heath Ledger. So, the same guy stars in both a movie as a homosexual and another as a Christian golfer? Really? I mean, come on God! Why does this have to be so difficult? I literally can't go anywhere without the reminder of my crisis of belief. It's absolutely unbelievable! Could I just have a day without feeling like a failure?*

I must note the irony of Jake Gyllenhaal's performance in the movie we watched. I find it hilarious that I was asked to watch a movie featuring the same actor from the gay movie *Brokeback Mountain*. I'm curious if there was any forethought by the staff at the facility. Some things seemed to go right over their head, while they were hypersensitive about other things. A perfect example was me not being allowed to have reading material "from outside." I wasn't allowed to read *The Girl Who Played with Fire* due to its secular nature, but it was totally fine for me to watch Jake Gyllenhaal's performance in a secular movie? Some things just did not make sense from a logistical standpoint.

DAY 21

*The book Katherine has me reading is called **Helping People Step Out of Homosexuality**. Included at the back of the book is information about a residential program. Their facility is located in San Rafael, California. It states, "Those who enroll in the Steps Out Residential Program can expect God to work on the deep wounds of the past. They must be prepared to allow God to bring breaking, cleansing, and new ways of living, which will result in a happier and more mature life. The program's focus is not aimed towards sexuality. Rather, it is designed to bring deeply ingrained non-sexual issues to the surface in order that the homosexual desires brought about by these issues might be resolved."[1] BINGO! That is why I flew to California! And yet, getting to my root issues is not what I'm experiencing. Why am I here and not there? I'd be able to get to the root of my problems. I plan on reading this to my dad to see what he thinks. I feel this other program would be way more practical and worthwhile. The real issue would be how much it would cost.*

THE "STEPS OUT OF HOMOSEXUALITY" program was pretty infamous. Later, doing research on its effectiveness, I came to find out that many individuals who have gone through Steps out of Homosexuality have reported experiencing trauma as a result. I am thankful I was not in this program. However, my preoccupation with it provides further evidence that I *really did* want to change my sexuality and behavior. I obviously wasn't seeing the promised changes at NH. My internal conflict was also reaching a boiling point and I wanted outcomes from my efforts. While my parents' primary reason for my being at NH was seeking life-based resolution (i.e., substance use control *and* sexual orientation change), I simply wanted the latter—something directly focused on sexual orientation change. Something more like, dare I say, the program Exodus International offered. Thank goodness Exodus did not end up being my program, though. I've heard much worse stories from survivors of Exodus's program than what I went through at NH.

> *"Train up a child in the way he should go; even when he is old, he will not depart from it."*[2]

> *My parents raised me up "in the way he should go." Yet I have fallen away. I have never left The Church or stopped spending time in Christian community. However, in my personal life I have fallen far away. This verse is a promise to my parents. I keep trying, though, and nothing happens.*

It is deeply painful to read how religion took me to the brink of risking my own sense of well-being. I thought I was at NH for that reason. It was why I asked to go into the program in the first place. I felt the need to be straight because the Bible said homosexuality was wrong. But given my experience and study, this did not make sense, so I wanted answers. Now that I am an out and proud gay man ten years later, reading this day's entry makes me feel deeply troubled and sad. It shines a light on how distorted my view of myself and God's opinion of me were. To suggest I was willingly choosing to be gay is now offensive to me. At the time, however, I felt I needed to believe I was being willful for my own salvation (and to gain acceptance and approval at NH). *That*, in and of itself, is the embodiment of religious trauma.

DAY 22

Marvin is leaving for Sober Living this week. Alex will soon be leaving for New Orleans. The only two people I can talk with and trust are leaving. Hunter is leaving this week as well. That leaves me, Kevin, and Ian. Ian seems to have Kevin under his manipulative spell. So, where does that leave me? Regardless, things are about to drastically change. I wish I could just get the help I need instead of jumping through hoops and dealing with all of this uncomfortable drama!

I MENTIONED HOW I feared losing my relationship with Marvin and Alex. Losing Alex was going to be difficult because of how connected he and I had grown over the course of my time at the facility. Marvin and I had experienced quite a bit of tension. Some of this tension was the result of me not wanting to be a so-called "team player," but some of it was genuinely the result of me feeling unappreciated by him. However, prior to Ian's arrival on the scene, Marvin and I had started to grow closer together and he was a familiar face.

Ian presented himself as a characteristically egotistical individual. I found it difficult to connect with him. He made feeling like an equal, something I had to fight for. What bothered me most about Ian was his pride, and it triggered something within me. Losing both Marvin and Alex around the same time, feeling unappreciated by Gavin, and strong-armed by Ian, ultimately made for a hostile environment. While Marvin and I were not as close as Alex and me, he was still a safe person.

> *Having been an intern at a State Hospital, I can easily detect Prison Mentality. Since Ian arrived, Kevin has started changing. In a way, he's acting like a shock collar in the house. Instead of addressing these issues in-group, he's privately coming to my room. First, he came by himself and then again with Ian. This kind of behavior is textbook Prison Mentality.*

I discuss "Prison Mentality" in today's entry. With this statement, I'm alluding to the impact a lack of autonomy can have on individuals in this type of facility. Prison Mentality can lead to people feeling they are in a constant state of having no choice, free will, or sense of privacy. To top this off, it causes one to feel the need to wear a mask to avoid being exploited, adhering to a stringent list of rules and regulations. This environment has implications for one's behavior, causing reliance on others to function (and therefore, a lack of autonomy/individualism). It may seem drastic to make the claim that NH was doing this to its residents but there were elements of this, given their amount of control.

DAY 23

I have a feeling this may be something God revealed to me. From a very young age, I have always sought the approval and acceptance of those around me. I didn't just seek it but had to have it in order to be okay. I'm unsure why. I remember I always felt older than my peers. I didn't always exemplify this in my behavior but often did in my thinking and understanding. People would often tell me I had an 'old soul.'

In previous entries, I have spoken about my religious spirit. I stated I embodied a religious spirit in order to deny my homosexuality. I do believe I have a religious spirit, but don't think it stemmed from homosexuality. I sought the approval of my classmates and got rejected. Due to my need for approval, I kept looking. In my search, I found The Church. My gifts and talents were easily used in The Church environment—I flourished and satisfied my need for approval.

My need for approval, when seeking it from man, doesn't end. It simply moves from one person to the next. When I left school, my need was back. I found myself spending more and more time at church, many times just by myself in the sanctuary. I wasn't sold out on Christ. I was addicted to approval and validation. From there, my religious spirit developed.

To continue from before, as soon as I left church, I was back on the prowl for an approval fix. I would try and try, but most of the time I was rejected. My life became miserable. One night while working at a fireworks stand, my schoolmate/coworker came on to me. *BINGO* My craving for approval was fulfilled. I consequently craved more and more of that approval, which translated into more and more sexual promiscuity. This continued until this behavior developed into an addiction. I was never gay. I had just mentally connected approval with homosexuality. I couldn't live without approval, so I couldn't live without being gay. Fast forward four years, and I'm at a treatment facility trying to get help. I have been such a fool! This makes so much sense! I'm not really a homosexual.

———◦———

To this day, I am still a validation junkie. I fully believe my need for validation began with The Church. Having been raised Southern Baptist, the fall of man and the sins of man were always at the forefront of my religious upbringing. Being told, "You are not accepted without God's intervention," and that "No one is good," created a type of havoc in my mind at an early age. Throw in the car accident at age six, and my mindset totally makes sense. I was a young, impressionable, and (quite frankly) needy child. I required extra tender love and care, and wholeheartedly believed everything I had been taught in church. When you believe everything The Church taught you without question, it results in a cycle of shame and guilt, requiring validation *from that church and its leaders* to combat it.

Looking back at my need for validation and patterns of behavior, my sexual encounter in high school was complicated. It combined my need for validation with my untapped sexual desires. For the longest time, I viewed the incident at work as sexual abuse—I needed a way to explain my same-sex attraction, as well as excuse my behavior. I truly thought it was wrong at that age. Remember, I was a Christian kid who did not drink, smoke, or engage in premarital sex until this point. Therefore, I needed an explanation as to why I would engage in such behavior when I clearly did not believe I was gay at the time. Analyzing that behavior from my current vantage point, I can clearly see how validation played a huge role. I wanted to be accepted so badly, and when the opportunity presented itself, I willingly walked through that door to find validation. This was coupled with finally recognizing my own repressed sexual desires. The link between validation and sexuality left me in a state of confusion regarding who I really was.

DAY 24

I called home and asked my mom to open my Facebook and send both Davis and my roommate Hunter messages. I was hoping to eventually schedule a visit with Davis, but it turns out he is in Afghanistan. I had my mom give Hunter my number since I don't have his. I am itching to know if WashU sent my acceptance letter. I called Michael and got caught up on all that has been happening at college. Michael was studying, which was no big surprise to me. The kid always has his head in a book. He informed me that some of our friends are dating again, which I think is awesome. I also gave Ethan a call. Yeah, I know, I may be in the wrong, but maybe not. He'd received my letter. I asked him to send me his own letter and fill me in on the details of his missionary trip. It didn't sound like he really wanted to, but we'll see if he does. I have my doubts.

GROWING UP, I HAD never felt really connected to my male peers. To be honest, it is still a struggle to this day. Part of this lack of connection lies in my own sense of insecurity and lack of confidence in socializing. I attribute some of my social difficulties to my traumatic brain injury. But to be fair, a large part of it is a result of my natural social awkwardness. Given the social difficulties at that period in my life, I was concerned about my relationships with my friends Ethan and Knives. Ethan and I had a history through Campus Crusade. As I described in the introduction of this book, a lot of my personal trauma originated with that organization. As a result, earning Ethan's approval was an important pursuit for me. In contrast, I viewed Knives as one of the coolest people I had ever met. I therefore wanted to really impress him. Now, ten years later, I do not really talk to either party. Are we surprised?

> *My mind has been centered on my friendships all morning. God can be cruel—this was evidenced when Matthew led a 'No More Excuses' group on marriage. This is extremely relevant for Marvin, Alex, and Ian but not to me. All this group did was mentally take me back to my relationship problems. I could not escape the regret I've been feeling all morning. I struggle in relationships. I've lost most of my friends and to add on to that, I've never been in an "official" relationship with someone of the opposite sex. I don't know why this is, but I've never had someone romantically interested in me. I can't imagine a girl being interested in me or wanting to be alone with me. Placing my struggle with homosexuality aside, I have serious issues accepting the thought of a girl in my life. My issue isn't that I wouldn't want someone, but that no one would want me. I know this statement reeks of self-pity but it's the truth.*

In addition to my difficulties with male peers, I introduced my insecurities in dating relationships in today's entry. Granted, I primarily emphasized my lack of confidence with women. I do not want to sound dramatic or like I'm throwing a self-pity party, but I have since resolved that I will likely be alone for the rest of my life. If something were to change and I were to find a man invested in me, I would be open to a long-term relationship, but I am not counting on it. I have honestly been alone for so long, I cannot imagine what life would be like with another person. I struggle feeling confident in people's opinions of me so my analysis or critique of my "dateability" from this day is still accurate. I do not believe I have the qualities needed to maintain a healthy romantic relationship. I have too much trauma and have been through too much. This may sound sad and depressing, but I am honestly okay with it. Learning to be okay with myself has been the hardest thing I've ever done in my life, and I don't expect anyone else to have to do that work on my behalf.

DAY 25

I knew I'd get to this point eventually, and I believe this is partly why I've been running for so long. I am a modern-day Jonah.

"Now the word of the Lord came to Jonah the son of Amittai, saying 'Arise, go to Nineveh, that great city, and call out against it, for their evil has come up before me.' But Jonah rose to flee to Tarshish from the presence of the Lord. He went down to Joppa and found a ship going to Tarshish. So, he paid the fare and went on board, to sail with them to Tarshish, away from the presence of the Lord." — Jonah 1:1-3

From a young age, I knew the Lord called me. I knew I was not to merely be a Christian but was called to do something specific for his Kingdom. Yet, I have been unwilling to fully submit. Instead, I began running, just like Jonah did. I've been searching for excuses, arguments, justifications, anything to get me out of what the Lord has required of me.

Like Jonah, I boarded a ship headed as far away from the presence of the Lord as I could get. In this analogy, the ship symbolizes same-sex attraction and my willingness to engage in homosexual activity. Satan worked his magic, pulled a few strings, and set the course of my destruction. I had plotted with the devil and received my reward. Like

Jonah, I boarded a ship, which at first traveled with tranquility, until the Lord brought a storm. Like Jonah I was thrown overboard, and I lost everything comfortable in my life. A great fish swallowed up Jonah, and I was sent to NH. I know the end of Jonah's story, what will be the end of mine?

Jonah spent three days and three nights inside the belly of that fish. While there, Jonah dealt with God. He surrendered his life to the Lord and handed over the reins of control. It took Jonah's being swallowed by a fish to follow the Lord's plan for his life. What will it take for me?

I had no intention of paralleling my life to Jonah. I hadn't even read it until I began writing and it came to mind. The Lord has been working on my heart all day. I know my time here is like the time Jonah had in the fish. I've been running for so long. God eventually got sick of this and had to throw me overboard so I would be forced to stop. Jonah became extremely thankful for the fish, so it's only a matter of time before I become thankful for NH (and as my writings reveal, I've been doing my best to prevent that).

The truth is, God always wins. It's just a matter of time. I've got to surrender. Merely saying the words, however, is not enough. I must hand over my rights: My hopes—My dreams—My future—My desires—My career—My relationships—My education—My intelligence—God wants my life.

That is a tall order—so tall it has me scared to death. I've been on the run because I feel it's too much. I've let God have bits and pieces of myself over the years, but I have never given Him my all. It's like jumping off a cliff. Over the last few days, the Lord has been diligent. He keeps calling me to lay my burdens at the foot of the cross. I've walked towards it but ran away. I then came back and then ran again. This is why my journal reads like that of a young man with diagnoses of bi-polar disorder and schizoaffective disorder. Back and forth, back and forth. God is calling. My heart is softening, and His voice is getting louder and clearer. I know it's only a matter of time before God breaks through and reveals some truth that will change my life.

———◦◦———

LOOKING BACK ON THE analogy of the Jonah story, it is clear I was trying to find something within the Biblical text through which I could relate my story. The story of Jonah corresponded with my storyline because Jonah ran from his problems. While in this program, the counselors repeatedly told me I was running from God. I felt the staff were trying to make me realize my own brokenness and need for God (thus proving my running from Him). They did this to justify their goal of turning me toward God through different means than what I'd tried before—I was clearly still gay, and my prior efforts had not worked. The Jonah story and my story had a direct parallel. Do I still relate to the Jonah narrative now? Hell, no. I do not. In all honesty, I was simply fishing for a way to describe my experience, so it made sense at the time. I was looking for a story that would parallel my situation.

Even though Hunter is staying for a while, the staff still held his graduation, as well as Marvin's. The graduations were somewhat engaging. Everyone went around and shared something. Love seems tangible at these kinds of gatherings. I easily get emotional, even when it's not about me.

The forms of love demonstrated at NH graduations are the closest I can allow myself to get to. I know I can't ever expect love on a personal level with just an individual or peer. I know I have individuals who do love me, but I feel incapable of receiving it. That is why I value gatherings like this so much. They make me feel like I am part of something, a brotherhood, so to speak. Just the thought of being accepted, valued and loved as part of a group of guys sends me into an emotional frenzy.

After the other residents' graduations, I noted the amount of love present in the room and the overwhelming sense of brotherhood. This feeling of love then, as well as now, is immensely powerful to me. Its power lies in the fact that I have not experienced a sense of belonging with other men for most of my life. This lack of platonic relationships with other men is something with which I continue to struggle. Feeling a sense of belonging is, at its core, what I need but lack. Without it I was, and often am, left to question my own ability to receive love from peers, specifically my male peers. Ever since childhood, acceptance from males had been a struggle for me, and this reality became evident during this meeting. Receiving the very thing I lacked revealed how much I needed and craved it in my life.

DAY 26

I met Katherine and my whole demeanor has changed since speaking with her. When I first got here, I approached her with the intention of getting "what I want." I wanted answers and expected her to tell me what I needed to do. Looking back, I am embarrassed at how arrogant and prideful I have been. I'm surprised she didn't immediately kick me out. I now approach her in a different way. I admit I still have moments where I return to a prideful state. The change has been subtle, but I am no longer hoping to have my problems fixed or my questions answered. I'm now in search of God and what He wants for my life. It's crazy, right?

Anyways, the meeting with Katherine was good. She asked where I am emotionally, and I explained the two primary things: 1) the social situation (Alex and Marvin are leaving and the Ian problem) and 2) God's work in my life (asking me to surrender my entire life and the call I feel is on my life). Here is a breakdown:

1) The Social situation

a) The absence of Marvin, and eventually Alex, parallels the relationships I've had in the past. I turn into a third wheel and am eventually left behind and forgotten. In the past, this would generally lead me down a road of bad deci-

sions. My feelings of abandonment and loneliness gave me an excuse to do as I liked. It may have begun with a drink but would usually end in the form of a random sexual encounter. Katherine listened and expressed compassion by explaining how this is the perfect place and time to deal with all that again. Except, this time, I have the opportunity to rise above and deal with loss by completely relying on and growing in the Lord.

b) I expressed my frustrations with Ian, and Katherine understood. She reminded me of things I have been striving to tell myself: 1) There is something within Ian that reminds me of myself, which is part of why his behavior bothers me so much. 2) When I first arrived, there were plenty of less-than-positive things about me. She did, however, validate my feelings of frustration. I shared how Marvin and Alex's absence and the influence of Ian on Kevin and Hunter is making me feel very alone. I can already feel myself isolating. I do not want to have a bad attitude, but I'm developing one. Katherine challenged me, saying this could very well be the Lord calling me to draw closer to Him. Instead of allowing my anger to consume me, I need to humbly come to the Lord. Just as God had shown me grace, He desires the same for Ian. It goes against my natural instinct, but I need to start praying for Ian—asking the Lord to work in his life. It's convicting but in a good way.

<u>*2) God's work in my life*</u>

a) God has placed a burden on my heart and is not relenting. I shared how I have never fully surrendered before the Lord. I have discussed this with Katherine before. I have also said and written it down on paper so many times, I myself am getting sick of hearing it. The Lord is asking me to hand over control of my life. I want to, I need to. God is calling me to let go, I just don't know how. Katherine encouraged me, saying it's clear I have been doing it and that I must keep seeking the Lord and leaning only on Him.

b) I also shared how my head knowledge feels like a curse. I can't get out of my head! There is a definite disconnect between my brain and my heart. My fleshly, carnal understanding is overpowering the spirit. I am struggling to get into my heart and to operate there, rather than operating in the worldly understanding of my head. As usual, Katherine spoke the truth: I've got to get into and live my life in humble reverence of the Word, allowing its application to impact my life. During our conversation, Katherine mentioned a scripture that scares me: "narrow is the gate that leads to eternal life, and few are those who find it." I want to be one of the few! But it all comes down to this: The Lord works in His own timing. Now is the time to wait on the Lord.

I DO NOT THINK I saw it then, but I can see it now. There was an elevated level of extreme spiritualization at NH. Katherine had a way of taking my past experiences of rejection, poor decisions, and trauma, and painting them through a Christian lens. She spiritualized *everything*. As a therapist now, I do not feel this was appropriate, clinical, or right in any way, shape, or form. No matter how positive my interactions with Katherine were, in her insistence to push everything through the lens of Christianity (rather than providing some much-needed support), I was left with a pervasive and constant sense of guilt and shame at the facility. It was not about what had happened to me, but what the Lord was having me go through to form me into the person He wanted me to be.

Put another way, whether on purpose or subconsciously, NH's "treatment" methods were controlling and about a need to be "right." The staff wanted me to say the things they wanted me to say and do the things they wanted me to do in order to reward me with the label of a "good and faithful Christian." In shaping me (and others) into the type of people they thought Christians should be, the staff at NH also received their *own* validation, as well as further evidence that they had been in the right in their treatment toward me. In reality, none of this really had anything to do with God, but everything to do with making Christians feel good in their "accomplishments."

Instead of addressing the real trauma I had experienced in my past or aiding me in improving my mental health, I was essentially being told to dismiss and spiritualize my emotional and mental health. I was not being asked to deal with underlying issues but was being asked to avoid them through their idea that God had it "under control" and would bring good from it.

> *I called home tonight. I tried to explain to my mom what the Lord has been doing in my life. As she often has done, my mom quickly reminded me of all my faults. She challenged my testimony by reminding me how in the past I have been manipulative, fake, arrogant, prideful, selfish, and deceptive. It was as if she thinks I'll never change. My mom told me all my head knowledge is a curse and I rely on that instead of surrendering to God. She really knows how to lift a guy up! What if she's right? I'm trying so hard to surrender! I feel like I've made progress, but what if it's all show? I think I'll hold off from calling home for a while.*

I need to address the phone conversation I had with my mother. I think it's fair to say we had a unique if not an especially enmeshed relationship. She would express her care and concern about an aspect of my life, and I would become sensitive and would emotionally escalate as a result. We would then feed into each other's emotions until one of us screamed at the other (typically me at her). In this conversation, I am sure my mother's motive for being so harsh was to encourage me to take the program and my relationship with God seriously. I received this information through a specific lens and attributed a specific value that was not truthful. I would press and force her to say things she did not fully mean, and off to the races we would go. I want to provide this disclaimer, as my mother is an incredible woman who has done more for me than anyone in the world.

DAY 27

I checked my voicemail and my friend Davis had left me a message from overseas! I feel that is a big deal. He encouraged me to get real before the Lord. He stated that for God to work in our lives, we must make sacrifices and experience pain. While the journey is hard, it will be worth it in the long run. He will be back in the California area in March. If I'm still here, I would really like to see him.

THE STATEMENT BY DAVIS that "for God to work in our lives, we must make sacrifices and experience the pain" was a typical perspective of my friend Davis. He was a military man and treated Christianity from that viewpoint. He was an all-in or all-out kind of guy. Taking spirituality seriously was something he believed in. Further, he believed that God rewarded "warriors." To be a warrior meant to be strong and fight against all odds for the Kingdom of God. This meant suffering and learning lessons at the cost of sacrifice. It is a bit extreme, but it was how Davis related to the faith. Applying this to my situation while in the program, I remember trying to take this to heart. I struggled, though, as I felt so much underlying guilt and shame. No matter how hard I tried to be a "warrior" for Christ, the same-sex attraction would not go away. And how does one act as a warrior while handicapped and trapped away in a treatment facility? I can remember pondering this late at night after talking to him.

We went to Oasis tonight. I was actually looking forward to it. I sat towards the back by myself. Steve was there and pulled me aside to share some scripture, and to encourage me to seek God. He's a good guy.

A guy shared his testimony. Although he is married, he has had sexual issues. The mannerisms with which he spoke and moved his hands screamed 'homosexual.' He mentioned how going through Step 4 of AA (which I'll be doing on March 7 at the beach) was the most difficult aspect of his recovery. He also shared how he was sexually molested as a kid.

Bingo! Into the self-pity hole I went. I was reminded of all the people I've let down, the shame and guilt of my actions, and how worthless my life has become. I sat down in worship and bawled. I didn't share in the men's group afterwards. I sat in the back of the van on the way back. I hid my face in my hoodie and cried the whole way home. Isolation sounds so good to me right now. I'm shutting down.

Steve had mentioned how Step 4 of AA was the hardest step he had taken, which was a reminder of the steps I would have to soon take. Step 4 of AA consists of "A searching and fearless moral inventory" of oneself. The entire purpose of the exercise is to examine one's character and resulting behaviors. Through this process, one is then able to name his or her weaknesses that contribute to his or her addiction. Due to the intensity of this step in AA, the staff at NH had their residents go to Pismo Beach. It helped provide a sense of perspective while doing deep inner work. While I was apprehensive about the work I would have to undergo, I will be honest and admit that I was really looking forward to going to the beach.

DAY 28

Thank the Lord, Jack is here! I never know what will happen when he visits. Morning meditation was one of the most intense we've had thus far. Somehow the group ended up discussing how I hate myself. I'm not sure how that topic came up, but either way, it happened. Jack stated a person can never fully recover until he stops hating himself, learns to love himself, and quits focusing on the past. I know this to be true, but I seem unable to accept and execute that. Jack expressed the answer to learning to love myself is within myself, and no one can help me or fix me or tell me how to get there. The journeys to self-discovery and self-acceptance are different for every person. I will never get better, be healthy, have good relationships, and quit sexually acting out until I achieve these ideals. This doesn't mean I should live a gay life, but it does mean I need to quit hating myself, reconcile my past, and accept myself for who God made me to be. To put it lightly, morning meditation was intense.

IT SEEMED THAT MY heart was being played with since I'd arrived at NH. On one hand, I was being shamed and guilted into believing I was living a life that displeased God. But on the other hand, I was being told not to hate myself and to accept myself. How does one do both, exactly? I know that in this entry I stated that "this doesn't mean that I should live a gay life, but it does mean I need to quit hating myself, reconcile my past, and accept myself for who God made me to be." Who decides who God made us to be? Scripture? Prayer? Other People? Discernment? There does not seem to be a specific answer, and this whole idea of "change-but-accept-yourself" consisted of conflicting messages and led to *so much* further internal confusion.

It's time to sort some things out. NH is a great place. Yes, it is helping me grow closer to God, become humbler, and become a better person. For that, I am very thankful. I owe so much to Christopher and Katherine, I truly do. However, one thing I know to be true is I am gay. There is literally no way of getting around it. I can put on a mask. I can pretend to be something or someone other than myself. I can do that. But is that the answer? Is that the solution?

I have three options before me:

1. I can continue to believe God's will is for me to be straight. I can continue to believe God can and will change my sexual orientation, which would bring God glory, make my parents extremely happy, and life would be temporarily much easier. If I go down this route, it is likely I will eventually marry a woman and father children. However, I would inevitably have to get a divorce because of my homosexual identity. Such a turn of events would destroy the life of said "future wife" and the lives of any potential children. Not to mention, I'll hate my life because of it.

2. I can accept I'm gay and believe it is God's will that I live as a homosexual. In doing so, I would utterly break the heart of my parents, receive rejection by most of the Christians in my life, and be misunderstood and judged by the conservative Christian church. However, I would be happy. This happiness would come from me being true to who I am and following what I believe to be God's will. If I go down this route and it is not God's will, I will be disobeying God and not reaching the potential plans He had for me in the beginning.

3. Being gay or not being gay may become too much and too confusing to figure out. Thus, to stay in the will of God, I will live my life single and alone. If I'm truly gay then I will live a depraved life, unable to fulfill my desires and what I believe to be fundamentally true about myself. My parents will be happy that I'm not living a homosexual lifestyle but greatly disappointed that I'm not married (i.e., no grand-children).

*The truth of the matter is, **I am gay**. I know this is the truth. I firmly believe the Lord has revealed to me that I was born this way. However, I am still living for, and on, the grace of other people. I can't be honest and express my true feelings because the staff here doesn't believe anyone is born gay or that being gay can be in God's will. Being honest will only result in me being embarrassed in groups and a longer sentence at NH. I also can't express this truth to my parents because they also don't believe these things. My hands are tied. I know I have written about this so much. I'm honestly sick of thinking about it, but nothing is changing. A few days ago, my mom told me to focus on my other issues, and I have been. In fact, I believe I've been seeing progress in those areas. However, my parents are really after one outcome: my becoming straight. They are spending a lot of money to get that outcome, yet I know for certain it is not the outcome they will receive.*

The question is not whether I'll break my parents' hopes and dreams but when. How long am I willing to torture myself and play this game? I've attempted to be completely transparent, but now that I believe I know the truth about myself, the transparency must end. Transparency means being stripped of my freedom and remaining locked up.

That being said, I do like it here. Other than pretending to not be deeply convicted about my sexual identity (I've been doing it for four years), I am growing and changing. No matter the outcome of my sexuality, I have gotten closer to God and less 'prideful' and 'arrogant.' I'm no longer begging to leave. I actually have no problem staying the full 90 days. Or at least, I think I have no problem. The only issue is, even if I stay that long, the outcome still won't be my parents' desire. So, sure, I can stay but it's only wasting my parents' money and postponing my life.

I went outside frustrated and angry. I began yelling at God out loud. I may have even used a few choice words. I promised to quit asking God 'why.' I don't need to know why. That's irrelevant. I got on my knees on the basketball court and lifted my hands in worship and surrender.

I then humbly asked for two things.

1. Direction. I asked for another confirmation of whether to accept myself as gay or to continue trying to change my sexuality.

2. Parents. If his will is for me to be gay, I asked him to work on my parents' hearts. I went so far as to ask God to have one of them initiate that acceptance. Asking that of God may be asking too much, but it doesn't hurt to ask. God is good and I believe He'll respond. At least, I hope He will.

After reading this day's entry, I feel mixed on how to translate The Church's view of the will of God vs. the actual will of God. In my opinion, there is a difference (and a significant one at that). Years after my experience at NH, churches in the United States often accept homosexuality, evidenced by churches accepting gay people into their congregations, professing that homosexuality is not a sin condemnable to death, and even allowing gay people to serve in ministry positions which had previously been categorically restricted. This proves the point that acceptance (or lack of acceptance) of homosexuality is based on a Church perspective more than a universal Biblical truth. As I discussed in a previous entry, there are valid arguments against every verse used against homosexuality in the Bible. When looked at critically, these six verses simply do not hold up as a means by which to reject homosexuals in The Church. However, conservative Christianity keeps a stronghold on safeguarding what is and is not acceptable for churches to embrace. Unfortunately, many gay individuals are convinced that The Church's perspective is God's perspective, which is *so far* from the truth. As evidenced in this entry, I was in that same boat.

DAY 29

We went to church at Calvary, and I intentionally sat in the back by myself. The pastor preached on Armageddon in Revelation 14. I tuned him out because I do not agree with his perspective. Instead, I turned to Jeremiah in my Bible and read that. One passage really stuck out to me. In fact, it may possibly have been God speaking to me about my prayer last night.

"I sat alone, because your hand was upon me, for you had filled me with indignation. Why is my pain unceasing, my wound incurable, refusing to be healed? Will you be to me like a deceitful brook, like waters that fail? Therefore, thus says the Lord: 'if you return, I will restore you, and you shall stand before me. If you utter what is precious, and not what is worthless, you shall be as my mouth.'" — Jeremiah 15:17-19

As the music began to play, I sat down, put my head in my hands and asked the Lord to speak. Something came over me and all I could think of was Option #3 (from yesterday's journal). This is the option I most dislike. I felt the Lord was revealing that He called me to serve Him—I am not to be with a man or a woman, ever. Thus, the issue of 'gay' or 'straight' is irrelevant. I felt the Lord was calling me to singleness and humble service to Him. I absolutely hate that option. I have been alone my entire life and have wanted to figure myself out so I could be stable enough to eventually date (whether with a man or a woman). I sat there and kept asking, "Is that you speaking? Is this me, or You?" I felt or heard nothing. I have a feeling my thoughts weren't my own because I would never willingly choose the third option. I fear the Lord has spoken and this is all He is going to give me.

As I sit on my bed journaling through this, I am reminded of what the Apostle Paul wrote:

"To the unmarried and the widows, I say that it is good for them to remain single as I am. But if they cannot exercise self-control, they should marry. For it is better to marry than to burn with passion." — 1 Corinthians 7:8-9

Perhaps I have been praying for the wrong thing. I've been praying for resolution in my struggle with homosexuality, one way or the other. Upon reading over this scripture, it's likely I should be praying for self-control and diminished selfish desires.

The verses prior to the above scripture are:

"Now as a concession, not a command, I say this. I wish that all were as I myself am. But each has his own gift from God, one of one kind and one of another." — 1 Corinthians 7:6-7

The ESV commentary speaks to these verses:

"The 'concession' refers to permission to refrain from sexual relations for short period of time. Paul does not demand such periods of abstinence, though he does permit it. 'Each has his own gift.' Both marriage and celibacy have their own benefits, and both should be considered 'gifts.' Paul is happy that God has given him the gift of being content with remaining unmarried, since this permits single-minded devotion to the Lord's work."[1]

The more I look into this, the more it makes sense. I know the Lord's calling has been on me for most of my life. I have fought against it in a variety of ways. My homosexual desires have been a thorn in my side for a good while. However, these desires may be null and void if the Lord has called me to singleness to make a difference in the world, and ultimately, bring Him glory.

I actually kind of like the sound of that. Jesus was single. The Apostle Paul was single. Mother Teresa was single—a pretty heavy list, yet all of them changed this world. Is God calling me to have my name on that list? I need to spend some serious time in prayer about all of this.

If being single is God's will, the singleness is an honor from God. I've been angry and upset with God. However, if he gave me the gift of singleness so I could bring him glory and advance the kingdom, then perhaps I should be thanking and praising Him!

THE THREE OPTIONS I laid out for myself were quite extensive, considering the various possibilities before me. The third option, to be neither gay nor straight, but to live a life of celibacy in honor of the Lord was the position I felt I needed to push myself toward. However, this position did not take *my own* real and actual feelings about my sexuality into consideration. It was what the program leaders, my parents, and the Christian church had said *they* wanted. But were their perspectives realistic, let alone healthy? Looking at things now, recognizing the shame and guilt maintained in telling me celibacy was the answer to all my issues, option three was not realistic, nor was it healthy. In fact, I would argue that their view was the definition of denial. One can only live in denial for so long before one gives in.

This does explain a few things. First, it makes sense why I'm not attracted to women. If God made me attracted to women and still called me to singleness, it would be kind of cruel. Second, I've spent twenty-two years of life without ever being in a serious relationship with a woman. Third, what do I make of this problem of homosexuality? The conviction that I was born gay kind of flies in the face of this call to singleness. However, if I wasn't born gay, some things do fit together. Perhaps, I craved intimacy so desperately I sexualized it. This is why I was already turned on even before my coworker touched me that night at the fireworks stand when I was in high school! I was so lonely, any form or prospect of intimacy triggered a sexual response.

From that point forward, I felt like any intimacy, even from a man, is better than nothing. Because God may not have given me attraction towards women, I've manufactured my own desires so I could receive intimacy. Over time, my desires solidified on the male gender, and I became an addict of intimacy. This explains my compulsion for random sexual encounters, as well as my tendency to cycle back into guilt/shame and church involvement. Even when I have accepted myself as gay, I have not desired a committed relationship with a guy. I just want a short random sexual encounter. In essence I took a gift from God, rejected it, and sought to receive what I thought I needed. In doing so, I've practically destroyed my life.

Sexuality and intimacy are two separate things, but what was the fireworks stand incident about? The incident at the fireworks stand in high school had triggered all sorts of confusion and questions about who I was and the kind of person I wanted to be. I do not think I was not initially attracted to this other student, but when I was offered the opportunity for some intimacy with another male peer, which I so desperately craved, I was incapable of saying no. Further, I think this experience did open the door to my true sexuality as it was the first homosexual experience I ever had.

DAY 30

Things within the house are still not okay. In discipleship class, Ian made the assertion that those who are spiritually mature do not swear. In saying this, he looked directly at me. This upset me. I had recently had an outburst of anger which included swearing. He sat smug in his chair and was making a claim that he was more 'spiritually mature' than me. Alex jumped in to try to salvage the conversation, but it had already derailed. I found myself in the hot seat. I know this is my pride speaking, but I would like Ian to wear my shoes for one day and live in this personal turmoil. He can then tell me I am "less than." I have been attacked and offended by someone who hasn't been here long, refuses to take responsibility for his own sins, and is playing one of the biggest and largest religious acting games ever! To make matters worse, Ian has manipulated everyone in this house. In a way, he has formed a party which judges and treats me differently. I am not comfortable here and feel strongly disliked. I am unsure of how to remedy the situation. All I want to do is curl up in a ball and hide. I refuse to be manipulated and pretend to be someone I'm not in order to gain acceptance. It may be prideful (I don't think it is) but I have integrity and I'm sticking to it. In looking at this, I don't think the situation is going to get any better anytime soon.

To combat Ian's accusation, I stressed that God is after our hearts. The Pharisees did everything right, yet Christ called them a brood of vipers. I stressed how God works from the inside-out, not the outside-in. Further, I pointed out that honesty is a sign of spiritual maturity, not a sign of its absence. Ian ended his attack at that point, but he did not back down. He then went into a diatribe about how he doesn't judge others and it is not his place to do so. By saying this, he was trying to receive praise for his convictions! This guy is one hell of a piece of work. All of this is seriously ruining my day.

I HAVE HAD A tendency over the years toward low self-esteem and lack of self-confidence. This lack of self-confidence often translated into a fear that others did not, would not, or could not like me. I have struggled in relationships ever since I was young, which I know now was affected by the traumatic brain injury. Out of a need to compensate for my weaknesses, I have always been a rule follower and held myself to an exceedingly high standard. Unfortunately, I would also expect others to hold those same values and standards. Ian fell short of what I found acceptable, and I believe he had figured that out. Once he figured it out, he was able to press my buttons. His lack of appreciation of me brought my insecurities to the surface. Further, the lack of validation or recognition by others of what was happening caused me to spiral. Therefore, I may have been a bit paranoid. However, Ian's actions were truly alarming from my perspective at that time.

When Matthew got to work, he handed me two letters from the mail! The first was from my dad, which he had told me over the phone to disregard. However, he wrote something profound. Here is an excerpt from my dad's letter to me:

"Here are a few of the things where we saw Satan try to destroy you this past year, when you were trying to do right.

1. You wanted to move into an apartment with others, as living alone was not good, then you move and what do you know! George is your neighbor! Do you think Satan had anything to do with that? (It could have been Christian boys living next door).

2. You wanted to go to a nice Halloween party and then instead, you were taken to a gay bar and eventually ended up in a threesome in the basement of Professor Mary's son's house. Satan again. [I have a lot of shame regarding this.]

3. You went to the S.S.A. small group at your church and then older guys were struggling mightily and no one was being victorious, hating their marriages, etc. No one gave you hope. Satan again."

For all the crap I give my dad, this was fairly insightful. He doesn't know the details of the Halloween party, however, he just knows it was bad. I wish he hadn't mentioned it. It is seriously painful to think about. I seriously fear my friend will never talk to me again. Ugh—I didn't want to go there.

I should speak about the events of the dreadful Halloween party all those years ago, speaking of insecurity. I had been dabbling in sexual activity with the worship pastor from the mega church at which I was interning. As a result, we had gotten quite close. During that time, he invited me to an event in a different city with a lesbian professor he knew. We were invited to a nice dinner with this professor and her wife. It was the first time I had ever been invited to an event with all gay people and felt like I could be myself and explore the gay community. I felt accepted there, and as a result, I felt comfortable and got drunk that night. From what I can remember, a friend later found me. I was in the professor's basement, engaged in sexual activity with people I did not know. My friend was horrified. I embarrassed and humiliated my friend and myself, in front of a professor, nonetheless.

DAY 31

Morning classes went extremely well. I honestly feel like the Lord was speaking to me. I felt like the Spirit was speaking to me through the discipleship material. To summarize, I felt like the material communicated that there comes a time when one gets fed up with their own beliefs and understanding so that they willingly set aside these things to learn what God had spoken. I could not have conceptualized this in a better way. This is exactly what is happening in my life. I've spent years trying to make sense of my life and have failed. I thought if I got my understanding right, my relationship with Christ would be right as well. I couldn't have been more wrong. I needed to slow my life down, genuinely seek after the Lord, become obedient to His Word, and everything else would fall into place. I had flipped the equation. It is imperative I continue to surrender and trust. Surrender. Trust. That is the key.

SURRENDER AND TRUST. I don't know how to describe what was happening with my mindset other than to call it brainwashing. That is certainly what some of this felt like. I had been convinced that not having same-sex attraction was equivalent to being obedient to God. And therefore, having same-sex attraction meant I was in opposition toward or against the purposes of God. Now, whether this was intentional on behalf of the NH staff or not, it was definitely implied. The conviction this placed upon me became so great I emotionally had surrendered myself to God. I'm not so sure that the staff were aware of my emotional posture. Regardless, the psychological gymnastics I put myself through because of guilt and shame about my sexual desires was immense.

Gavin later had us sit in a circle and give compliments to each other. It was great to hear—I'm curious if what said was actually said in honesty. The group lasted one and a half hours!

I find it intriguing that with all the details I have included in this text, I neglected to include the compliments given to me by my peers. Especially when I was just previously feeling hated, disrespected and unappreciated. It's almost as if I wanted to dwell on the negative. I think there is a part of feeling exhausted and powerless in which one stops focusing on any aspect of the positive and finds comfort in the negative. I think that is where my mind was at this point in the journey. I wanted the negative because it helped fuel my anger and justifications not to engage. I wish I could remember this day and the things that were said but I do not.

Christopher showed up this morning and announced that Ian was moving to the other house with Marvin, Alex and Gavin. I became very upset, so Matthew called me into the office. According to Matthew, the move had nothing to do with me and Ian was not being promoted. Looking at it now, yeah, I'm upset it wasn't me, but it isn't that big of a deal. I am still living in the main house, so I don't have to walk a quarter of a mile every day to groups. Now Marvin and Alex have to deal with Ian. Haha! It's actually funny. I can't wait to hear their stories!

I approached Ian for a discussion. I cleaned my side of the street in relation to him and that's all I can do. Ian refused to take responsibility, blamed our dissension on Satan, and asked for me to respect him. He said I hurt him because I wasn't receptive and hadn't quickly become his friend. I find this unbelievable. After hearing what he had to say, I'm glad he's moving down to the other house. While I still have to endure him in groups, at least I will have time away from his B.S. at night.

Ian wasn't loud or disruptive, but he was a presence to behold. That is to say, Ian had a way of drawing attention to himself when he wanted it, and diverting attention away from himself when he didn't. Looking back, what I remember most about Ian at this part of the journey was his manipulation. He was smart, coy and devious, and he knew how to play NH' game. He would act certain ways around staff but then a different way when they were gone. He made rude and snide comments as well as used facial expressions to allude to things that were often inappropriate or out of pocket. Ian was a character that was difficult to manage and created challenges to deal with as a fellow resident.

DAY 32

I received two packages in the mail today! My mom spent some money and bought me a Renovare: Spiritual Formation Bible! I'm so incredibly thankful! There is one downside though. She ordered the devotional-sized one. I asked for this specific Bible because of the commentary. The text is so small, it is tough to read, but I don't care. At least I've got one! The other package was a box full of goodies: four blue G2 pens, two black G2 pens, one specialty G2 pen, three highlighters (it's clear that my mom knows me well), dove chocolates, an edition of Time magazine and two books: Life Without Limits and a book Jackie recommended, Mending Cracks in the Soul. My mom also included a copy of two days from her devotional that had direct application to a card, and an encouraging letter. I'm telling you what, I don't deserve to be treated so well. I am so thankful!

I WAS REALLY ENCOURAGED to receive mail from my parents. I remember that receiving mail while in a facility really brightened my spirits. There was nothing quite like it. Given that my mother and I had recently had an argument over the phone that had quite offended me, I think this was her way of apologizing. To this day, she will do things like this. When we get into arguments or she knows I'm having a hard time, she will go out of her way to do something for me. Sometimes, I think she does this because she feels guilty for her own actions but for the most part, I believe that these actions are motivated out of love.

> *Gavin gave us more time to work on our Bible studies. I'm amazed by how much depth I'm discovering in Jonah. There is so much to unpack in merely four verses! I feel the life of Jonah closely resembles mine. My time at NH parallels Jonah's time spent inside the big fish. During that time, Jonah waited on the Lord, repented of his sin, and gave God thanks. So it is with me.*

> *I asked Gavin if I could give my Bible study instead of doing Every Man's Battle group. He said yes. In my talk, I asked the question, "What has God called you to do?" and "Why are you holding back?" I stressed how the question is not if God will use us, but when and how? It's up to us. We can keep going around the mountain, but the Lord will always bring us back and we'll be faced with the decision again. I don't know if my study was any good, but man, I love speaking in front of people.*

Prior to entering NH, to this day, I am a pessimistic kind of guy. I typically view the glass half full. However, in order to survive this program and in order to try to find some salvageable good out of what was being taught, I approached the program with a "what is redeemable?" mindset. Therefore, even when things were very negative and discouraging, I would try to see the positive. It was a survival technique that got me through the program.

DAY 33

Bob arrived and brought some convicting material with him. I feel it's appropriate for me to work through it, due to its direct application to myself and things I need to change. I feel the content is paramount to my recovery. However, I only have time to work through two of the points. I feel the following are the most important. I will only think about the others instead of journaling about them:

FIFTEEN STYLES OF DISTORTED THINKING[1]

1. Filtering: you take the negative details and magnify them while filtering out all positive aspects of a situation.

... This has been a serious problem for me, especially in relationships. I always assume people think the worst of me and continually find myself justifying my actions. By always assuming the worst, I began to strive for and rely on the validation of others. I must learn to find my validation and acceptance solely in Christ. In doing so, I will not have to be concerned with what people think of me. I won't need to filter out the bad because it won't matter!

2. Polarized Thinking: things are black or white, good or bad. You have to be perfect or you're a failure. There is no middle ground.

... This is so me! I struggle to roll with the punches. In the past, I've always viewed things as black or white. If I stumbled, especially regarding sexual sin, that would be it. I screwed up and all my hope was gone. I must learn that even though I mess up, I am not a failure. I need to learn how to rebound.

THE SECTION IN DAY 33's entry on filtering and polarized thinking is strange to read now as a Licensed Mental Health Professional. Filtering and Polarized Thinking are common cognitive distortions, and I would never offer the solution to this thinking as an intervention in finding validation in Christ. Rather, I recognize the ways in which our brains run to make sense of the world—how this can often become misconstrued, leading to faulty thinking. Cognitive Distortions are common. Most people deal with them often, even daily. Having knowledge of their presence in our life allows us to adjust our thinking, but relating them to spirituality in no way serves as a healthy strategy.

During my session with Katherine, I confessed I had called Ethan. I feel bad because I didn't tell her I had also called several others: my brother, cousins Billy and Jeremy, and my Aunt Kelly. However, while I feel bad, I think I'm okay—I am no longer going to call anyone until I have her permission! Under normal circumstances, this would mean I would lose phone privileges. Apparently, Katherine appreciated my honesty. Instead of taking away my phone privileges, she is allowing me to use my iPod. I know that this is not a normal thing nor is it a right. I also know it wouldn't have occurred without full staff support. I feel honored and very thankful.

It's amazing how having my iPod during breaks has improved my mood. Being able to listen to Jason Upton, Matthew West, Tenth Avenue North, and Skillet draws me closer to the Lord. I don't know how to explain it. It's weird, but simply being able to listen to that kind of music in between breaks strengthens my connection to God. I know that sounds silly, but it's the truth.

I couldn't help but look—I found an open wireless connection and found checking Facebook via my iPod too tempting, so I did. I already feel extremely guilty about it. I'm going to speak with Matthew about it tomorrow. If the staff think checking my email is unacceptable behavior, I'm perfectly okay. I must remember using my iPod is a privilege, not a right. I pray by giving in and checking my Facebook, I haven't lost this privilege. I know that I must come clean, confess, and leave the rest up to God.

I do not think the staff were aware my iPod was able to access the internet. I'm almost positive that if they were aware I had this access, I wouldn't have been granted permission. If I wasn't allowed to read *The Girl Who Played with Fire*, I certainly wouldn't be approved for unmonitored internet access. Therefore, when I discovered the local network, I felt thrilled and like I had a secret to keep. I know that I should not have used the local network to access the internet when this was explicitly against the rules. I know this, but the temptation at the time was far too great.

DAY 34

I woke up feeling off. I wanted to fast but without any form of caffeine, my brain refused to operate. We went to have our TB tests read this morning. Before leaving, we did our chores. I got down on my hands and knees and scrubbed the floor. Kevin kept bossing me around, which did not improve my mood. At the clinic, I was found clean of TB. No surprises there.

On the way home, Matthew stopped at Target. He had me go in with him to pick a movie. As I browsed through the options, it became apparent my normal picks would not meet NH restricted guidelines. I wanted to choose The Tree of Life, but it was out of stock. No surprise there since it's such an amazing movie. I thought Abduction and/or The Social Network sounded good but Matthew did not approve. I handed the choice over to Matthew and he picked The Craigslist Killer. That wouldn't be my first choice, but I wanted to see it, so I was down.

I WILL NOTE THAT 'The Craigslist Killer' seemed a peculiar choice for the residents of a Christian drug and alcohol rehabilitation facility. However, I'd seen the staff make weird decisions regarding what was and what was not allowed or restricted before. As a result, I went along with Matthew's suggestion. That being said, it certainly would not have been something I would have encouraged residents to watch if I were a staff member. Why? Because it had absolutely nothing to do with recovery and quite frankly, wasn't exactly appropriate for the setting.

> *On the way home, we stopped by Christopher and Katherine's house. Christopher brought out a bunch of signs. Each sign has only one word, but together the signs read, "Jesus Is the Messiah. Real Men Pray." And one sign read, "Honk If You're Saved." I didn't jump out of the van, so Christopher assigned me to hold the cross—he had made a literal cross. I actually like that. I think he will have us stand on a sidewalk somewhere, perhaps before or after helping the homeless tomorrow—I don't know.*

Sign holding seemed to be an idea concocted by Christopher. He was always coming up with ways to evangelize and get the guys involved in the program to participate in Christian events. I feel that holding a cross and waving signs asking people to honk for Jesus on the side of a street is a bit extreme, but that was Christopher's M.O. Just wait for *the incident*, because looking back, I find that entire encounter somewhat traumatic. Instead of processing it here, let me do that in tomorrow's entry. Read on!

DAY 35

After hanging out at the river, we went and held signs. Several of the homeless joined us, which was cool. I started by taking pictures. About fifteen minutes in, I gave my camera to Jack and took the cross from Hunter. Instead of standing with the cross, I got on the sidewalk on my knees and put the cross on my shoulders. At first, it didn't really influence me, but as I heard honking, people yelling for us, and seeing some people smile, it made it all worth it. Before long, I found myself praying for the people driving by. Christopher had his truck on with Christian music blaring in the background. Within thirty minutes, tears were rolling down my face. I felt humbled, honored, and loved. The call to absolute surrender overwhelmed me. I was thankful I was holding the cross away from the signs because Ian was running up and down the sidewalk yelling at the people in the cars. It was embarrassing, but since I was holding the cross, I didn't have to worry about it.

We received a great response. In fact, as I was holding the cross, I saw a woman stopped at a nearby light. Upon seeing us, she turned to her two teenage girls and began speaking to them. Before driving off, I saw her lift her sunglasses and wipe away a tear. I thought that was cool. Seeing that meant a lot to me and had an impact on what I was doing.

THIS SIGN WAVING AND cross holding experience was borderline traumatic. I'm finding it difficult to explain the reasons why it might have been traumatic, but at its most basic level, I was vulnerable and susceptible to influence. I was willing to go along with the event and even get down on my hands and knees holding the cross. I can distinctly remember crying, holding the cross, praying and asking God to intervene in my life, believing that God would act.

This expectation for intervention was really what made *the entire program* at NH (sign holding being a microcosm of this pattern) traumatic. The staff instilled a constant sense of anticipatory expectation and belief that God was going to do something big, that He was going to act. Waving signs and holding a cross in front of the public put me in a position of surrender and left me feeling powerless – wanting to experience the change I so desperately craved.

Looking back, I'm confused as to how the sign holding had anything to do with my recovery. It's like when we were forced to watch Christian films. If the staff could classify something as Christian, it was acceptable, regardless of whether it furthered my steps towards sobriety or heterosexuality. To top this off, I remember finding the experience more humiliating than it already should have been, given Ian's behavior of running up and down the sidewalk yelling at cars. Further, it's possible that there was an additional layer of emotional manipulation in that it was used to motivate change within us.

DAY 36

Jack had given me the paperwork for the Celebrate Recovery Steps 1-3. It's funny. I've been here for over a month and I'm just now getting this? William got his last packet last week and he's been here for less than two weeks. Is there a reason I was kept back?

———◦———

I WAS NEVER PROVIDED a reason as to why I was provided the Celebrate Recovery Step Process later than others. I'm assuming that the reason for the delay was because they felt I wasn't ready. This, I can only assume, was based on a continual back and forth dilemma between thinking I was meant to be in this program and wanted to change my sexuality vs. feeling like I was wasting my time and God had truly accepted me for who I was as a person. I wasn't exactly quiet about how I felt.

On the way to church, Christopher told Alex he should apologize to Katherine. Apparently, Katherine was upset about us going to The Gate. Alex had asked Christopher if he could go before he left the facility and went back home. Why does Katherine feel uncomfortable having us at her church? And why are we treated like children when we go?

We were instructed to sit together in front of Christopher and Katherine so they could monitor our behavior. I'm an adult, thank you very much. I have successfully completed four years of college, and have been accepted into the Number One Social Work Graduate School in the country, but I can't be trusted to behave in church? You have got to be kidding me!

Besides my obvious irritation, I loved The Church service. The worship session was incredible. Charismatic was one way to describe it, but it was also solid and based on Scripture. Right up my alley. One song went "We live in the power of God/ to break chains." Hands raised, eyes closed, I felt the Lord assuring me He has the power to break my chains and set me free. All I must do is press on, wait, and trust. That was worth the last month at NH put together. Now, why aren't we allowed to go to The Gate on a regular basis? That kind of worship could be the key to my recovery. I can't get that kind of experience at Calvary.

It's difficult to find a way to describe this without sounding egotistical, but I felt a special bond with the leaders of the program, Katherine and Christopher. I feel this was due to my level of educational experience and maturity. I felt I was able to relate to them on a level many of the clients could not. As a result, I felt it was reasonable and acceptable that I should be allowed to attend Katherine's church. However, the way Katherine and Christopher treated us when we *were* allowed to go, made me feel less-than. Ironically, this is the last thing anyone should feel at a church service. I never heard about clients acting out at her church, but it honestly would not have surprised me. In fact, it might explain some of Katherine's decision making. I personally felt like I was an exception.

DAY 37

This morning, I met with Melissa, a client service advocate in conjunction with the Sexual Assault Services. She began our session by describing her role. Her focus was not on my being taken advantage of by my coworker, but how that incident and its repercussions impact my day-to-day life now. (Sounds like social work to me!) We did, however, process through what happened. I was unsure if this encounter was simply experimentation or sexual abuse. After hearing my side of the story, she said it was indeed sexual abuse. I explained my reason for coming to NH, my involvement in ministry, and my switch to Social Work due to my homosexual desires. She explained that such a switch is not logical since I am a Christian—that sexual sin is the same no matter what career I choose. She cut to the point, and I could not pull my "feel sorry for me" act. I quickly gathered that conversation with Melissa is not going to be easy.

Melissa quickly detected a pattern to my behavior. We explored my disappointment in how my dad didn't meet my emotional needs. As a result of his emotional detachment, I would spend time with Aunt Kelly. After my experience at the fireworks stand (and following encounters) in high school, I learned I could temporarily meet my emotional needs through sex. However, this form of fulfillment was only temporary, just like my time with Aunt Kelly was

117

temporary. My homosexual desires, then, aren't my actual sexuality but mere fantasies of what could be another emotional fix.

When things went down in high school, I was not in a good place. My perception of the abuse felt positive. Given all the negatives, the positive experience became a comfort in the form of homosexual encounters. We explored the exhilaration and hope that came from experiencing such encounters. At the root I had no intention of having a long-lasting relationship. Thus, the route to change comes in exploring things outside of my norm, doing things which may seem uninteresting or uncomfortable. Melissa suspects that my natural inclination is to only do things I find comfortable. I am a man of habit and comfort. My comfort has been found in seeking out men for sex. In order for lasting change to occur, I must not only abstain from homosexual actions but also change my interests and way of living.

Melissa brought it all back to God and the Bible. She encouraged me to get some scripture memorized and under my belt that I can start proclaiming over my life. She reasoned that my situation is not about homosexuality, but rather, if I will serve God or not. She encouraged me to take a stand either way. Until I take an unwavering stance, there isn't much anyone can do to help me. She also mentioned that she detected a critical and judgmental spirit in the way I talked. I found that discouraging because I thought I had been working on getting rid of it! She explained that such a spirit will make change difficult, and I must get rid of it. After our session, she talked with Gavin and scheduled another meeting. I'll be seeing her again next Monday at her office.

The meeting with Melissa encouraged me. I have been living a pattern. Therefore, my behaviors and the trajectory of my life can be changed by changing the patterns by which

I live. I resolve to quit protesting the homosexual issue but rather, to embrace a new way of life based on what God says, directs, and wants from my life. My life before January 1 had become predictable and operated in a distinct pattern based on what happened in high school. However, while that experience has all but destroyed my life, it doesn't have to continue to wreck me. With God, I can rise above and live a new kind of life, a life characterized by freedom, love, purity, and healthy relationships. Heck, I might be able to be happy. Now that's an idea!

———◦———

IT WAS OBVIOUS MELISSA was initially vetted by Katherine and Christopher. From an organizational perspective, I would expect a treatment center to do their research about their providers and know the perspectives of said professionals. Having said that, I think Katherine and Christopher did more than simply understand her perspective. Melissa's assertion that "My (Seth's) situation was not over homosexuality, but rather, if I would serve God or not," revealed her true viewpoint. Rather than focusing on acceptance of my identity, she pointed me back to Christ. This was NH core *modus operandi*. This is sadly, a negative effect of religion—not being able to see the forest for the trees.

I spent years believing the sexual encounter I experienced with my coworker in high school is what "made me gay." I primarily believed this to be the case because I couldn't understand why God would have made me gay when I had been diligent from a young age in serving him. It didn't make sense to me, and I needed something to explain why I had these feelings and attractions. However, after having worked through my own journey of acceptance, I have moved beyond this point of view. I do not believe this one sexual encounter caused me to become gay. I believe I *was* and *am* gay regardless of this encounter.

(For those that may have forgotten, or not read the introduction, here is a brief synopsis of what happened between a classmate and I in high school):

"*I was working a summer job at one of those big pop-up tent fireworks stands during a summer in high school ... One night at work, we were sitting on top of the tent, watching to ensure the fireworks stand wasn't being robbed. I don't recall the topic of conversation, but I do remember there was a lot of sexual tension in the air, and this felt new and exciting. I hadn't done anything or said anything to encourage this tension, and hadn't made any physical advances, but I certainly wasn't discouraging the electricity between us. At one point, without warning and without my asking, my friend reached over and grabbed my crotch.*" After this incident, I became acutely aware that I was attracted to other males).*

DAY 38

It's now around 6:30 am and I'm in Pismo Beach completing Step 4 of Celebrate Recovery. I took a nap from 2:00 am to 5:00 am. I think I am almost done, if not completely finished with my moral inventory. I addressed my resentments, fears, sexual harm toward others, and non-sexual harm to others. My resentments and fears have made it onto a third page; however, the harm sections do not even fill one page. I don't know how that is possible. I keep wracking my brain and I get nothing. I'll talk to Jack this morning, as he may have some ideas. If not, I think I'm done.

Psalm 25 was on my heart all night and I spent the rest of the day with it on my mind. A few verses are:

"Turn to me and be gracious to me,
for I am lonely and afflicted.
The troubles of my heart are enlarged;
Bring me out of my distresses.
Consider my affliction and my trouble and forgive all my sins."

— Psalm 25: 16-18

———◆———

THE HARM SECTIONS WERE difficult, likely because I did not view myself as a person who was harmful to others. Coming up with ways in which I had non-sexually and sexually harmed others was a bit of a challenging task. With the way this activity was structured I felt as if I should have a lot of things in this section. However, when you think about it, not having parts of my life to contribute to this section was a good thing. It made sense given who I was along with my background. Given my perfectionistic nature, I wanted this completed in totality with nothing missing. I wanted all my bases covered.

DAYS 39–41

I was supposed to prepare my inventory for Jack in the morning, but it got pushed back. Christopher left early to speak to people in prison. He came back around twelve with an older gentleman named Rudy who came to present his testimony. It was obvious he had done these many times before, but it was good. His message, based on his life, was that finding your identity in God is paramount. The person you find (romantically) attractive will be just like you. One should therefore get to work embodying and practicing the qualities they want in a partner. God is faithful. So, stop playing games. His testimony was full of good stuff, but I can't remember it all now. I do remember it was a good encouragement before reading my inventory to Jack.

THERE WAS A PHRASE I often used in ministry when I was interning at a megachurch. I used it as an illustration with kids all the time and it went like this: "You can't fly with the eagles if you're running with the turkeys."

I know it's basic, but it supports the point that who you spend your time with will determine your future. This message echoed Rudy's speech. In my present-day life I still believe that who you spend time with plays a role in your future outcomes; however, I believe life is much more complicated. There are additional factors needing to be considered. Put simply, the outcome of one's life is multifaceted.

I have lived my life in self-pity and have used this self-pity to justify my behavior. I have allowed things that have happened to me to instill jealousy, envy, and self-pity. In doing so, I've lost my identity and have become a coward. I've taken the easy route at every single turn. The only reason homosexuality became a problem in my life is because I allowed it to be.

Jack and I went into Christopher's room in the afternoon. I was somewhat nervous. I had taken my inventory very seriously and it had very personal details in it. I made it through my resentments easily, but as I began explaining my fears something came over me. It's one thing to identify and write out fears, it's another thing to share them out loud with someone else.

About halfway through my fears, Jack stopped me. He's not supposed to say anything, but he did. Jack smiled and said I had answered all the questions I've been asking since I've been at NH. He told me it's apparent I was raised with good family values, but I chose not to live by them. Instead, I've dwelled in self-pity and used my intelligence to justify my actions and consequentially, dug my own hole.

The reason I am where I am today is because I've been a coward. I've been selfish. I preferred to be rescued from the hole I've dug rather than to climb my way out. Essentially, I refused to be a man and chose to live a life of self-pity, jealousy, and envy. The issue is not conversion therapy but balls and integrity. Although he wasn't supposed to make recommendations, Jack challenged me to try and be straight for five years. I think it's a good idea.

When Jack and Christopher were adamant that my sense of self-pity was the core issue of my homosexuality—that I needed to simply "man up," I believe I responded neither out of anger nor depression. Rather, I believe I stuffed these feelings down and allowed the excitement of the trip itself to overtake me. Stuffing my feelings had become a specialty of mine, until of course it no longer worked. Coincidentally, it was one of the reasons I had ended up at the program in the first place.

> *This is the deal: I am going to commit five years to sold-out faith in God. In doing so, I will not engage in homosexual actions. I will spend the next five years bringing my desires, confusion, and self-pity to the Lord. If, after this period, I am still unhappy and still feel the unwavering urge towards homosexuality, then I will embrace that lifestyle.*
>
> *I honestly do not believe I will be unhappy at that point. Seeing all the Lord has done in my life since January first, I have faith God will continue to work. But, having the stipulation that if all else fails then I can return to homosexuality gives me motivation. I can tell myself I only have to do this for five years, and then I can do whatever I want. While I say this, I have faith that it won't come to that.*

Upon reading about the five-year plan ten years after the fact, I literally laughed aloud. That I was seriously considering going five years being completely celibate was a bit ambitious, to say the least. However, reading this plan does paint a good picture of where my mind was at all those years ago. I was very much under the influence of a type of brainwashing. I was convinced that with "The Power of Jesus," I could do anything. Within the safety of the sheltered environment of NH, this all made sense. Unfortunately, in the real world, I know it does not really work that way.

DAY 42

We kept to the Friday schedule, which meant, movie day!
We watched the Experiencing God video. This time it was
about "adjusting your life to God." It was appropriate to
hear after doing my moral inventory. It's time for me to
make some serious adjustments in my life. If I am to be
successful at abstaining from homosexual behavior for the
next five years, there are going to have to be some major
changes: new and different friends, new ways of coping, new
hangouts, close relationships with Christian community,
participation in a local church and daily time with God
through prayer and Bible reading. Essentially, my way of
life must change.

THE PRIMARY CHANGES THAT were being recommended seemed to
include things like adjusting my social network, new life strategies, more
wholesome locations for having fun, close Christian community, vibrant
Church life, and personal time with the Lord. One could ask, "What
did any of this have to do with homosexuality?" and "Outside of the
Christian indoctrination of it all, wouldn't these choices be good for
anyone?"

I understand the necessity of changing environments due to the potential for temptation. For example, if I was going to leave a homosexual

lifestyle, continuing to hang out with gay friends and frequenting the local gay bar would probably not be helpful for the desired change in my sexuality. It makes sense within the context of my journal. However, these actions were benign in and of themselves.

It's hard for me to recommend religion to anyone. However, millions of people can engage with religion without it traumatizing them, experiencing positive and healing outcomes. I want to give credit to the fact that religion can be a healthy choice for some. The point, however, remains. These planned changes were not specifically targeting any homosexual orientation change which was critical to changing my lifestyle.

DAY 43

Jack led us in a group entitled "Letting Go." There were seventeen points, but they really all said the same thing. I think they can be summarized by number sixteen: "To let go is not to regret the past, but to grow and live for the future." That was the whole point of my moral inventory. It's time to let go of my grudges, fears, and guilt so I can fully focus on Christ, and look forward to the future.

THE PHRASE "LET GO" was a bit of a cliché in this treatment facility. From Christian messaging to Christian Recovery Meetings, "Letting Go" rhetoric was continually repeated with utmost veneration. However, it didn't make sense for me to "let go" of my homosexual lifestyle before I had been able to work through the childhood trauma with Melissa—especially when the program was insisting the trauma was what had caused me to become gay in the first place. This sheds light on why I wasn't asked to go to Pismo Beach earlier during my stay. However, the staff had me come and work through the steps at the same time I was unrooting childhood trauma that supposedly contributed to my homosexual behavior. How was I to let go? And what was I letting go of? I think more than anything else, what they were after was a commitment to celibacy, and that's why the staff deemed it time for me to go.

DAY 44

Matthew stopped by and handed me a letter from my dad, which touched on several things. 1. He encouraged me by saying, "Short-term pain for long-term gain." 2. He is concerned that I think I can still drink in moderation (My history of alcohol has led to homosexual behavior, the idea is no alcohol=no gayness). 3. He tried to convince me that real friends wouldn't tempt me to drink.

I really appreciated his letter. I called home and my dad shared that Katherine e-mailed him back. She said she will call him tomorrow. She also said she wants to talk about specifics—she has some concerns my parents should think about. Hearing this makes me think she is against me leaving that early. My dad didn't think so, but I guess I'll find out what she thinks tomorrow. I talked with my mom and apologized about my attitude yesterday. Somehow, alcohol entered the conversation, and we had a bit of a disagreement, but overall, it went well. My mom informed me they would be coming to San Diego on March 1ˢᵗ or 2ⁿᵈ for a meeting. They are planning to either pick me up then or visit me. Either way, it'll be so nice to see them!

After the call, I sat on the couch with William and Jack. I shared the debate I had with my mom over alcohol. Jack laughed and shook his head in disbelief. He stated that I was still on Step 1: Denial. I tried to argue my way out, but

*I know I am lying to myself. I am personally convinced that
I shouldn't mess with alcohol, and I really have no plans to
do so. However, I do enjoy arguing it for the sake of principle.*

———○———

IT WAS STRANGE THAT I was in a drug and alcohol rehabilitation center,
but thought it wasn't a requirement for me to commit to being fully
sober when I left. However, this incongruity highlights the differences
between what my parents and I had in mind for the program's outcomes.
It became clear that my parents' expectation wasn't just for me to become
straight, but to become fully sober (considering the damage it had caused
in my life prior to entering). I, on the other hand, believed I could focus
on the *cause* of the excessive drinking, which was same-sex attraction.
Once the issue of my homosexuality was resolved, I assumed I would
automatically have a healthier relationship with alcohol. My parents,
NH, and I had different perspectives. Taking these altering views into
consideration, my father didn't fully understand the causal nature between alcohol and same-sex attraction. I believed that same-sex attraction
resulted in drinking. My father believed that drinking led to same-sex
attraction. Thinking back on it now, I truly think my intuition at the
time was right. Drinking had been a coping strategy I used to handle the
devastation of being gay in a Christian hetero-normative world. Now,
was there *any* truth in assuming my same-sex attraction led to substance
use? I don't think so. In fact, I would argue the two weren't related that
way at all.

DAY 45

Matthew took me to meet with Melissa. I shared how our previous discussion lined up with my moral inventory. I have been living my life in a pattern. Melissa challenged me to begin setting boundaries, specifically boundaries for when I will be tempted to act out. From there, I shared how terrified I am of being alone. At the same time, I am terrified of being rejected. I generally stiff-arm people and test them to see their trustworthiness. The tests are typically silly but include things like reaching out for support and seeing if the person responds. If they do, for how long and what is the response? If they don't respond quickly enough or respond in the wrong way, they fail. These tests are generally unreasonable and beyond what most people could pass. When people fail my tests, I feel bad about myself and pursue a hook-up to make myself feel better. We discussed how these tests aren't necessarily a bad thing. In fact, they are a coping/self-protection mechanism. However, the result of people failing tests feels undesirable. I need to learn a different way to handle such disappointments.

Melissa wanted to know more about my fear of being alone since it has had such an impact. I have shared my insecurity with both the Christian community and the gay community. I went to Christian friends for help, but they didn't know what to tell me, or how to act around me. My honesty has scared many of them, making them not want anything

131

to do with me. Relationships weren't much better in the gay community. My desire to change pissed most of them off. People made a point to let me know their feelings. I felt almost as much animosity from the gays as I did the Christians. I don't think my sin is worse than others. I fear I will be rejected, and no one will understand what I'm going through. I do not have confidence in myself, and regard others as better than myself. I fear I will not measure up. Since I hate to be rejected, I keep people at a distance.

My fear of rejection has turned inward and is evident in how I talk. When I find myself attracted to another man, my negative thoughts about myself come out. I am quickly persuaded by the Devil's lies that I am no good, I am a terrible person, and no one loves me. Once these thoughts run their course, I enter a deep-seated place of self-pity and want to prove I am loved. I discovered the quickest way to prove I am loved is through sex.

Melissa challenged me to take my negative thoughts captive. I must reach a point where I both understand and believe the truth about myself instead of the lies. Once I claim authority over who I really am, I must proclaim this authority over my life. In doing this, I will fight Satan's lies and schemes to destroy my life. If I can become successful in this fight, I won't need sexual encounters to validate my worth. Before leaving, Melissa gave me homework. I am to write out all the different positive truths about who I am before our next session.

I struggle to accept this perspective. Having been obsessed with sexual bondage and homosexual addiction, I want a complex solution. The process given by Melissa seems so simplistic, it actually offends me. That being said, her perspective is logical and fits my story. I'm sure her theory is ultimately correct. However, there is a part of me that hopes she is wrong.

INSECURITY HAS BEEN A struggle for me ever since I was a young kid. I'd like to say I only tested developing friendships when I was younger. However, if I am honest with myself, I continue to conduct this relationship test from time to time—just not to the same degree. I have never had a lot of self-confidence. Think of my high school experience. Rejection has always been something of a negative force in my life. With rejection comes a pervasive sense of fear—a fear I am not good enough. This sense of inferiority has been something I've continued to struggle with. I just don't test relationships as brazenly as I did prior to my time at NH. To be honest, before the gay conversion program, I tried to keep up my friendships and maintain a vibrant social life. Now I just accept being a loner and am okay with it. Regardless, I understand that to test friendships to verify loyalty is unhealthy and manipulative. End statement.

Jackie came to do a group, and I was very excited. The Holy Spirit tends to show up when she is here, and I could use some Holy Spirit today. Alex began the meeting by playing his guitar. I've heard him talk about playing for over a month, but this is the first time I've been able to hear it. He didn't pick a specific song, but just played and picked strings. It was beautiful. Alex allowed the Spirit to do as he saw fit with his music.

I closed my eyes and swayed back and forth. During this time, I did my best to give up control and surrender my will to God for the night. I want so badly for me to get out of the way so that I can hear from God, be set free from bondage, and be healed. This was what I prayed for while Alex played.

Jackie began the group with a lesson. Using the book, 'Mending Cracks In The Soul' as a reference, she discussed the entrances into our lives that Satan typically uses. She began by using the acronym: T.R.U. C.O.P.S. However, Jackie only had time to explore the letters. T and R. They represent "trauma" and "rejection." Trauma shatters a person's soul, and as a result, hardens their heart. Rejection, on the other hand, causes a person to turn inward and experience internal pain.

Jackie asked me where I was in my progress. I explained how my first meeting with Melissa correlated with the moral inventory I did at the beach. I explained my patterns of self-pity, excuses, and justification. Jackie said my life has been under manipulation by Satan and he has plotted some serious schemes to destroy me. She pulled out my intake form, asked permission to share it, and proceeded to read it to everyone in the group. As she read the description of my family, she asked the group, "This sounds like the perfect family, right?" She mentioned my personal issues needing acceptance, love, and approval. She commented, "Isn't it kind of strange how Seth describes his family as a great family unit, but at the same time, struggles to feel accepted and loved?" I explained how I have always felt pressure to please them, to be the kind of person they want me to be.

From there, things got awkward. Jackie opened the floor for people to express love and compassion toward who I really am, not the person I want to be. I began to cry as Kevin, Alex, William, and Matthew, all gave me sentimental compliments. I struggled to wholeheartedly receive it.

Jackie asked rather bluntly, "Do you hate your father?" I responded by saying I am deeply disappointed with him. Growing up, I wanted a dad I could be close to, one who showed personal interest in me. My dad failed to meet both of those needs. Jackie said she suspects I experienced some rejection from my dad prior to my being six years old. I do not remember this. But, as a result of this rejection, no matter how hard I try to change, I never will until God sets the little boy inside me free. The pain from my childhood, Jackie believes, is the source of my low self-esteem, my desire to meet others' expectations, and my fear of letting people down. I need to learn to accept myself for who I really am and break my co-dependent relationship with my parents. Before leaving, Jackie gave me homework to write an angry letter to my dad.

The gay conversion therapy model is founded on a hypothesis that homosexuality must result from the relationship between a child and his or her continually distant father and over-meshed mother. I was searching for answers, was in a vulnerable state, and was ready to accept any explanation I was given to explain why I had the feelings I did. I legitimately didn't understand why I had same-sex attraction. Within the Christian framework, I didn't understand what I had done wrong growing up in The Church. It therefore makes sense why Jackie would move in the direction of *"I hate my father."* Ten years later, I do not believe my father ever rejected me. Let me repeat this: *I do not believe my father **ever** rejected me.* In fact, I fully and fundamentally believe my father has always been a present person in my life. He may not be a deeply emotionally connected type of man, but when it comes to dependability and love, my father takes the cake.

DAY 46

After morning meditation, we did our chores. We didn't do any groups because of the graduations. Ian's graduation was first. It felt awkward because I didn't have much to say to him. I gave a basic compliment on the depth of his biblical knowledge and understanding, which is accurate. He does know the Word. We went around the room, and eventually it was Christopher's turn. I was surprised by what Christopher shared. He did not offer Ian any compliments, but subtly implied that Ian is narcissistic. Christopher gave him a jab for being over-spiritual with his sermon to the homeless. I almost felt bad for Ian. It's possible I have said or done things that might lead Christopher to say similar things to me at my graduation! At the end of the meeting, Ian gave a mini sermon. This was typical, but it wasn't that bad. He focused on talking the talk and walking the walk.

I HAD A LOVE-FRUSTRATION relationship with Christopher while at NH. On one hand, I absolutely loved Christopher's passion and his inspiration. The man was full of energy and ideas. On the other hand, some of his behaviors were very frustrating. He was often unpredictable. Therefore, while his words about Ian were surprising, I was not all that surprised when Christopher said what he said to Ian. Saying these words at his graduation, however, did seem odd. I do not know why Christopher waited until Ian's graduation to share some hard-hitting truths.

I called home and had a good conversation with my parents. My dad talked with Katherine today. He said she only had positive things to say. In fact, she stated the changes in my life have been remarkable. In a way, I'm a success story. She told my dad she truly believes I will be used by God to do mighty things. For this reason, she is careful what she says around me. She is not only influencing me, but also the people I will help. I found those words extremely encouraging. However, (there always seems to be a "but"), she doesn't think I should leave just yet. Since she sees potential in my life, she wants me to get the most out of the program and become as solid as possible before I go. I don't like that response, but I know it's true.

My dad also informed me the staff will be watching me very closely for the next few weeks. Alex flies out tomorrow morning. My best friend will no longer be here. Loneliness used to be a trigger leading to partaking in alcohol, marijuana, and sex. How will I handle it? What will I do to compensate? What will my mood be like? In the next year, there will be times I will feel alone, lonely, and things will not feel ideal for me. Experiencing those emotions and learning how to cope with them while I am here will be very important. If I can't deal with it in a healthy way while I'm here, there is no way I will be able to handle it in a healthy way in the real world.

I mentioned I would most likely be moving to the other house and would likely become bored. I can't remember if my dad said Katherine commented on that, but I think he did. If I move to the other house, it will be another test. How will I respond to more freedom? Will I still make God a priority? What will I do with my free time? What will my mood and attitude be like? I suspect all the free time will make it much harder to stay motivated and strengthen my desire to go home.

All-in-all, I think these tests will be good for me. I look forward to them, since they will force me to decide between God or myself. I must put God on the throne, not just in my talk, but also in my walk. Bring it on!

Moving to the other house would obviously come with additional freedom and fewer interactions with others. The first house was my comfort zone, and I was used to my life there. I remember being excited about the pending move to the new house. But I also feared I would miss my parents more and wouldn't receive the same level of care. Not being around others would inevitably make me even more homesick. Also, being away from the main facility with a lack of supervision would increase temptation to engage in sexual fantasies and lust. The staff were essentially handing over free reign over a fortress, saying, "Here you go, Seth!" This was kind of weird when you think about it. Here they were, just heating things up in the program and then giving me near-complete freedom.

DAY 47

With both Alex and Ian gone, the atmosphere in the house is changing, once again. Interestingly though, the change wasn't entirely negative this time. William and Hunter (yes, even Hunter) were more open and talkative. Maybe I wasn't the only one affected by Ian. However, the important thing is I like the changes I'm seeing. In fact, I actually woke up feeling kind of spunky this morning.

I'm experiencing a sort of freedom. I don't know, it's like I've been set free. Simply put, I feel I've come out of my shell. (I'd say "closet", but I have already done that! Ha-ha. Gay jokes. I'm funny). Seriously though, it's like a weight has been lifted. I'm talking, I'm sharing, I'm encouraging others, and I'm reading my Bible. Weird, right?

I RECALL IAN'S LEAVING the facility made me feel as though a weight had been lifted. It seemed everyone felt a shift in the environment, not just me. Yes, I was most certainly grieving the loss of Alex, and this was an intense emotion of its own. However, Ian had held a solid grip on the emotional atmosphere of the facility. When he left, it felt like the auditory relief of a vacuum cleaner switching off. For the first time since Ian's arrival, other residents felt willing to share without fear of judgment or criticism. It was like people could breathe again. I therefore felt the positive impact of Ian's absence at once. Coming to terms with Alex's departure, however, would take more time.

DAY 48

Katherine and I reviewed last week's lesson during our meeting. She helped me brainstorm an entire page of "sights, smells, and sounds" that are reminders of the gay lifestyle. All of these details make it difficult to not want to return to the lifestyle. They could be considered "triggers". In order to be successful in the future, I must learn how to submit these triggers to God, so I don't end up running back to my old life.

Before the end of the meeting, Katherine said something that set me off. The following events only confirmed my feelings. What was a good day has now turned ugly. I know I must rise above and be an adult, but I need to let loose.

My dad forewarned me that Katherine planned to share an outline of changes they hope to see before I leave. I was looking forward to and excited about this! I expected a detailed outline of potential situations (Alex's absence/moving to the other house/etc.) with anticipated behaviors (peace/positive attitude/good coping skills/responsibility/etc.). You never get what you want or expect at NH, however. Katherine did not provide such an outline. Instead, she listed more meetings with Melissa, more meetings with Jackie, and reunification with my parents. I already knew about these things other than the last one. This outline changes nothing!

Further, Katherine prefaced her plan with "These are the things we want you to focus on for the next thirty days, not to say you'll be leaving, or these things will end after thirty days." I'm such an idiot. I was hoping to be encouraged and given a future date I could look forward to leaving. I guess I am too messed up. My exit date has been extended to some unknown date, which is further than I can see or imagine. I must live here day in and day out, never knowing when I'm leaving, and carry on with a smile on my face and a positive attitude? This is my life, not some small matter! I understand the importance of how I handle things not going my way, but using my exit date to test my character is not ok or fair! I kept these thoughts to myself, and I did not voice them to Katherine. You can't win over administration with logic, and it's best for me to keep my mouth shut.

I WAS FURIOUS WHEN Katherine presented me with an outline mostly listing things I was already doing—a visit from my parents being the only addition. I was hoping for and expecting a detailed list of practical activities or actions I could use as a way of speeding up my exit from the facility. No such list was offered. There were literally no practical applications to my current or future life. Further, with no way to speed things up, there was no established end date to look forward to. There seemed to be no light at the end of the tunnel. I felt hopeless in my situation. NH's refusal to give me an end date and extending my stay raised questions about their intentions. As a patient, it was probably a bit unfair for me to project my reasoning onto them. Katherine and Christopher didn't strike me as greedy individuals, but I suppose financial reasons could have been part of why they were hanging on to me. It was equally likely that they sensed I wasn't changing as quickly or as thoroughly as they'd hoped. Therefore, they may have wanted to keep working with me for a longer period in the hopes that something might "click" for me.

I didn't mention this in the journal and quite frankly, I don't remember why the staff restricted my phone access. However, I think they found out I had been calling people I was not supposed to be calling. If they had discovered this, that would have been reason enough to limit my phone access.

DAY 49

Jackie came and met with me. I had not yet completed the "angry letter to my father" she had assigned. It had been one of my goals for the week, but I had not found the time to complete it. I began the letter, but only wrote a little with a lot more to say. With all that had been happening in my life, I didn't feel that angry at my dad anymore. Jackie would not have any of that. She explained that if we have a splinter in our arm, we can't simply put bandages on top of it and expect it to heal. In order for healing to occur, we must first dig out the splinter, removing the debris. She explained it is the same with hurts and pain from our past. While I may not feel the pain or want to address it, I must go there if I ever want to feel whole and live in peace.

Through prayer, Jackie invited the Holy Spirit into the room. I asked God to dig up pain and memories I may not have even been aware of. I let go of control, and I found myself standing in my parents' garage. My dad had just been let go from his job as a salesman. All his work material, notebooks, legal pads, and documents had been thrown in the trash. I was in the garage searching through it all and taking out what felt like "gold" to me. I remember my passion for producing something important. It was weird, but the very presence of a large stack of paper exhilarated me (and still does to this day). There I was, searching through the trash when my dad walked down the stairs. He con-

fronted me, scolded me, and told me what I was doing was "stupid" and "wrong."

I was a small child and I craved to be like my dad. Since he had often been away because of work, somehow playing with his work materials made me feel connected to him. My "Type A" personality had kicked in, and I wanted to organize his stuff on my desk and pretend to be a businessman. Even at a young age, my desire to be around books and to become a famous writer were present. My father's criticism hurt me. He did not validate who I wanted to be, and this sent a message that I couldn't be like him. I internalized this as rejection and adopted the idea that something was wrong with me.

Another memory came to mind, and I found myself standing on the sidelines of a flag football game. I was trying to tell my parents I didn't want to play. My dad was standing there with his arms crossed and looking in the other direction. My mom was on one knee and telling me I needed to play. She said that normal boys play, so I must play. I stood there crying.

I was a little kid and didn't want to play sports. I would rather have curled up in a blanket and read a book. But no, I had to play flag football. My dad wouldn't even look at me. My mom was comparing me to all the other kids on the team. Who I was and how I felt didn't matter. I needed to be like everyone else. Not playing sports was not normal and I needed to be normal. It became apparent there was something wrong with me, and my identity was invalidated.

The Holy Spirit then took me to my kindergarten classroom. I was sitting playing with blocks. I was happy. This was something I enjoyed doing. The Spirit opened my eyes as a little boy in that room and Jesus Christ was sitting across from me. Jesus was smiling as well. In fact, he was laughing. I was laughing as well, as Jesus placed another block on the tower I had built. I felt secure, accepted, and comfortable. I could be me and it was okay. I placed one more block on top of Jesus's block and the tower crumbled. I smiled and looked into the eyes of Christ. He grabbed my hand and whispered, "I love you."

Suddenly, I found myself with my friend Meredith. We were five or six years old, and we were performing songs. It was a safe environment, and both our families were there (my mom, Stacy, Cherie and a few of Meredith's aunts: all women). Meredith and I were making up stuff as we went along and were acting silly. I was having fun. I was happy.

Jackie paused this memory and had my present-day-self walk into the room. I picked myself up. I looked myself in the eyes and told myself, "Tough roads are ahead but don't give up! You are special, and God has big plans for your future."

I then asked my younger self if I believed in Jesus. Little-me laughed and smiled and said to now-me "Of course, I believe in Jesus. Jesus loves me! Do you believe in Jesus?"

Time-out. My five-year-old self just asked my twenty-two-year-old self if I believed in Jesus. If that's not trippy, I don't know what is! The Holy Spirit opened my eyes once again, and Jesus was there holding both of my selves. Jesus looked at my twenty-two-year-old self in the eyes, patted my back and said, "You finally get it." Jesus smiled. He laid his head on my shoulder and we watched my six-year-old self play in my arms. Jesus smiled, placed his arm around my shoulder and said, "You have been set free Seth."

At this, I opened my eyes. Tears had been rolling down my face, and I kept having to wipe my nose as snot was accumulating. Regardless, I was in shock. I could not believe what had just happened. I felt safe, secure, loved, valued and worthy. I didn't feel the need to impress anyone, meet anyone's standards, or pretend. I was just me and I felt okay in that. I've never felt this way before. In a way, I felt as if I had just become a Christian. My past identity was now gone. I had been washed clean. In fact, I don't know who I am. My old identity has been wiped clean. All I know is I am a child of God and I want to serve him.

As I HAVE STATED before, part of what was problematic about my treatment at NH was that there had been *some* psychological validity to Jackie's therapy approach. However, with Jesus mixed in the middle of it, there were all kinds of unnecessary biases and influences based on spirituality. The events I recalled during this spiritual encounter/experience mostly consisted of things that had really happened. What's telling is, Jackie built all of this up emotionally with prayer. The spiritual momentum of prayer combined with the psychological motivation of wanting something to change made me recall meaningful (and painful) events. It was surprising how immediate the recall was for each event, each incident coming to my mind like a flash of light one at a time as I processed each. It was actually pretty trippy in that regard.

Jackie and I processed the experience. She asked if my parents exemplified the Jesus I had just encountered. My answer was no. This is not to say they don't know Christ, because I know they do. I wonder though, if they have ever experienced the same thing I just did. If they had, maybe things would have been different. I don't say this to place blame upon my parents, but maybe my life can be a witness to them.

I explained that throughout growing up, a very strong religious spirit was present in my home, my family, and my church. Jackie commented that she had never encountered a religious spirit as strong as the one that had taken rein over my life. Jackie warned me that with a spirit this big, it will not be easily given up. I must be prepared to combat it. I can expect strong retaliation from this fight and must be prepared. Right now, however, I'm enjoying the freedom and deliverance (yes, that's right, I've been delivered) God gave me. I feel whole. I have peace. For the first time, I feel truly forgiven. I am secure. Thank God! My responsibility is no longer to please my parents but to please God.

I mentioned having a "religious spirit" in this entry. I'm a bit surprised it was just then being addressed, as it had always been a concern of mine. I worry it's one of my least attractive traits. While I've been through a social work education and am trained to treat all people with unconditional positive regard, I continue to struggle with being judgmental toward others. At this time in my journey, a rather large struggle of mine was self-righteousness. To conceptualize what a "religious spirit" is, think of the Pharisees in the Bible. Common traits include pride, self-righteousness, legalism, perfectionism, condemnation, and division.

DAY 50

We went to serve the homeless. We went to the park and planned on setting up there. After talking to Frank, we changed our plans and went to our usual spot by the river. A group of guys we'd met at the park joined us. They seemed all right but gave me a weird feeling, so I kept my distance.

While we were there, Frank and I went on a walk through the area. According to Frank, Becky and Tony had attempted to steal Frank's generator. As a result, Frank threatened Tony by placing a knife to his throat and demanding he leave the camp. Becky and Tony had packed up shop and were gone. Parole officers and policemen had since come to investigate the area. Frank is not being charged, but several other homeless men were arrested for possessing pornography, alcohol, and in one case, an armed weapon. Many homeless individuals were avoiding the river area for fear of the police.

I allowed my conversation with Frank to take its course, and quickly found myself in social-work mode by starting to problem solve and offer practical solutions. Frank confided that he had molested his 6-year-old niece and has been overwhelmed with daily guilt. Frank's confession affected me in a really strange way. I spent the rest of the afternoon in isolation. While my sin is obviously far less devastating than child molestation, I feel just as much guilt as Frank.

149

When we got back to NH, I sat around the house dwelling in self-pity. My entire situation aggravates me.

————◦————

THE ENCOUNTER WITH FRANK on Day 50 was clearly a trigger for me. I was working in the role of a helper at the homeless camp, but at the same time also seeking help for myself at NH. Given what has been reported in some of the current news there have been subsequent assumptions made about the link between homosexuality and sexual abuse in The Church. While I have never been an instigator of any form of sexual abuse, the link of pedophilia and homosexuality constantly depicted in the news and other influential sources made me feel extremely uncomfortable. There has been a historical movement that has worked to criminalize individuals in the LGBTQIA+ community for decades, and I didn't want to find myself swept up in this mob mentality.

DAY 52

I got to talk with Katherine for a little while. I explained how I was feeling this weekend and how I should have handled it. We also discussed my exit date. She reminded me how when I first got here, I wanted to leave but eventually surrendered control and got over it. She reasoned that I had reached another point where surrender is again required. As a result, I must deal with it. Hearing her talk in such a manner made me feel like a lab rat. No lie.

Katherine then went on to explain that while in the program, I have been growing. I arrived here at a particular level and as I have worked on my life, new levels have been achieved. With each new level, more things have been revealed to me. At each level, I have been working on what has been revealed. Duh—that's all-common sense. Katherine then shared that she believes I have more "levels" to obtain. We had this conversation in her living room while her kids ran around the house.

DEFINING "DEATH TO SELF" is central to the entire Christian message. It's implicitly embedded in the idea of being 'born again.' As 2 Corinthians 5:17 states, *"Therefore, if anyone is in Christ, he is a new creation. The old has passed away; behold, the new has come.* "To suggest that the old has passed and the new has come is to suggest an inherent death to self—a sacrifice and change in behavior. Put differently, my understanding of death to self from a religious perspective is to forgo worldly desires that are selfish, physical, and egotistical while simultaneously turning toward Christ and wholeheartedly seeking his kingdom.

At the time I was in this program, I still had strong religious convictions. I therefore bought into this "death to self" rhetoric hook, line, and sinker. Now (more than ten years later), I view things quite differently. I'm not going to delve into where I stand in my relationship with Christ at this time, but I will say that much of the "death to self" rhetoric is in fact, religious manipulation sought from the oftentimes-selfish angle of The Church. The care and concern of the individual, their feelings, how losing their identity for the sake of Christ might affect them, their past trauma, and other factors, are typically ignored. Being repeatedly told "Who you are, and how you feel, don't matter" is extremely detrimental and damaging to the mental and emotional well-being of those seeking to find self-fulfillment, meaning, and truth within The Church.

To expound on this, once a seeker finds themselves fully involved and established, the notion of "death to self" becomes more about one's dedication to their given Church, than anything else. The things one church/denomination might say to "die to" are things directly in opposition to ideas, beliefs, and tenets of another church. If The Church is going to make recommendations for, and influence truth-seekers' and members' life-altering decisions, it is fair to scrutinize and criticize the motivations and outcomes from congregation-members' resulting actions—*particularly* when the physical, emotional, and psychological well-being of individuals are impacted.

DAY 53

We had a "No More Excuses" group, and the topic was about marriage. I have a history of mentally checking out during these conversations. I tried to stay engaged and get something out of it today. This discussion centered on how men are to treat their wives and meet their emotional needs. I can relate to some of this. If I'm honest, I'd love to be in a relationship with a woman.

Wait. What did I just say? Wow. I really just said that! It's the truth, though. I feel I know who I am and have gained a sense of security from Christ. This comes with confidence, and with that confidence I am saying I would love to have a girlfriend. I would enjoy caring for her and meeting her emotional needs. I know I could do that. As an emotional social work student, I know I have the emotional part of a relationship handled. It's other stuff that could pose a problem. However, I know with God's strength, all things are possible. (Even having sex with a woman? I think so.)

I FELT I COULD meet the emotional needs of a woman based on a prior relationship with a specific girl from high school. Based on this prior dating relationship from my teen years, I imagined I had the ability to provide compassionate and caring emotional support in a romantic relationship with a female. In high school, I had dated a girl named Jennifer. In our relationship, Jennifer and I were close, but we never really got involved physically. Physical intimacy would have been my biggest concern, had it gone any further. I felt I could handle dealing with emotions. Sex, on the other hand, was an entirely different matter. From the way I was talking in this entry, I had all but convinced myself I could stomach physical intimacy with a female with God's power. I hate to say it (sorry, ladies), but this was not going to ever be the case.

> *I've held my tongue and kept from writing this, but Gavin is getting on my last nerve. I requested permission to read The Lord of the Rings, and Gavin is hesitant in letting me. He believes the series is satanic! Is that not the dumbest thing you've ever heard? I am shocked, actually dumbfounded by this mindset. I just completed a religious studies class on the Lord of the Rings two semesters ago! I have studied the books in light of the gospel! I can't handle such a narrow-minded, fundamental, and legalistic perspective. It flies in the face of everything I believe in and know about God.*

I never learned the underlying conviction leading Gavin to conclude that The Lord of the Rings books were satanic literature. My guess is that because wizards and Orcs were included in the narrative, Gavin viewed these books in the same way as Evangelical Christians often interpret Harry Potter (i.e., Demonic). It's really quite silly, and in essence, a misunderstanding. Tolkien was the key person responsible for bringing C. S. Lewis, the famous theologian, to salvation in Jesus Christ. Tolkien and Lewis were best friends. They also had dueling opinions on how fiction should be written. Lewis believed in direct allegory where specific characters in the Chronicles of Narnia represented individuals from the Bible. Tolkien, on the other hand, did not share this view. He believed there was power within each character, wherein they had the ability to be positive or negative—to be different characters at different times in their story. Turns out, I still have some knowledge from that religious studies class. I could have (maybe should have) taught Gavin a thing or two.

DAY 54

Matthew took me to see Melissa. I like my meetings with Melissa but am always unsure of how to act. She catches every word I say, and I'm never sure of where she wants me to go during a session. I have been hoping to obtain a game plan and create coping mechanisms I can use when faced with homosexual temptation. Today Melissa explained she believes such coping mechanisms are surface level. She stated she believes my problems are deeper. She explained she sees a pattern in my life:

I am always trying to please others and live up to their standards. I experience emotions I feel I am unable to share with anyone else, so I suppress them. I do what is expected, then move about my business, all the while carrying those emotional burdens. When these burdens become too great, I collapse under the pressure. When I collapse, I emotionally shut down and isolate myself from others.

All of this sounded similar to what I have been doing with Jackie. In my sessions with Jackie, I have been trying to deal with 'burdens' and 'emotions' so I can be freed from the 'pattern,' as Melissa likes to put it. I didn't explain all of that, but I did discuss how I believe I have moved past it all.

Melissa asked me how I was going to convince my parents I have changed. So, together we compiled a list of things I have learned from my past, as well as new practices for the future. At the end, she described this list as my "NEW LIFE" and essentially, the coping mechanisms I have been requesting.

MY NEW LIFE COPING MECHANISMS

* Boundaries
* Scriptural Support
* Knowledge of Support System
* Recognize Healthy Relationships
* Feel Comfortable in Myself
* Able to Verbalize What's Important
* Accountability
* Personality Change
* Sponsor
* Financially Responsible
* Relationship with God

Of all the counseling I've received, this session was the best and most productive of them all. In the process of compiling this list, there was a lot of laughter and I felt completely comfortable. I like her approach because it's one hundred percent Social Work. Due to my college studies, we have a lot of rapport which really lightens the mood. Melissa even disclosed that I am one of her favorite clients. That made me smile. I found the session very encouraging, and I returned to the house with a new vigor.

My positive mood was quickly smashed by a few comments and judgmental rulings by Gavin. I tried not to let this get to me, and I avoided him. I spent some time with William and Hunter outside but kept my discussion with Melissa to myself. I don't want to do anything that would jeopardize or diminish the hope I received today.

THINGS WERE A BIT confusing in what was happening and being said between two branches of NH. First, in the treatment program, I was being taught to be a "good straight Christian". Then there was therapy, where I was being told not to feel pressured to live up to others' expectations. There were contradictions. Melissa had to be aware of this discrepancy if I was. For sure, she knew I was in a treatment facility to try and change my sexuality. I talked about it every session. Even then, in my brainwashed state, my undue level of confusion caused me to continually hit the pause button. I went forward through the program, but I can remember a part of me shut down because all these contradictions didn't make sense.

DAY 55

Bob led a group on the roles in dysfunctional families. I am unsure whether my family is "dysfunctional." No family is perfect, but I don't think my family falls into the dysfunctional category. Whether we do or not, I identified with several roles. In elementary and high school, I was the "lost child." I was passive and would intentionally withdraw. I did this because I didn't want to deal with the rejection I experienced in school and with my dad. I spent most of my time in my room reading and watching television.

In college, I became the "hero." I hoped exemplary achievement in school would solve my problems. I worked hard, and believed academic success would make me feel better. It could also possibly cause my dad to take interest in a relationship with me. I couldn't be the son my parents wanted, but if I was successful maybe I could be good enough. When it became clear that even those efforts would not measure up, I became the "scapegoat."

As the scapegoat, I felt trapped. There was nothing I could do to win over my dad's approval and affection. I rebelled by exhibiting hostility and doing all the things I knew were wrong. I started frequently drinking, occasionally smoking marijuana, and began sexually acting out with men on a consistent basis. It was at this point my parents sent me to California (at my request) to become the son they have always wanted. It's kind of twisted when you think about it.

After Bob's group, I met Katherine. To my great displeasure, our topic was my dad. We discussed all that went on internally this last weekend and processed several aspects of my relationship with my father growing up. The first area we explored was how I have acted toward my father. We determined I've been a smart-alec, disrespectful, rude, have made snide remarks, have been angry, cocky, arrogant, prideful, judgmental, and have felt justified in all of the above. Next, we explored the feelings I experienced growing up with my father. I've felt rejected, thought he hasn't cared, felt he wouldn't listen, have seen him as distant, cocky, arrogant, prideful, authoritarian, and have had a sense he thought he was better than me. Katherine asked how I've typically felt after interacting with my father. I have felt guilt, shame, disappointment, depression, and anger. Katherine asked how these feelings have impacted me. I have felt resentment, have questioned my own progress, have asked the question, "Has this all been for naught?", have felt like a hopeless case, have feared loss of privileges, and have been hard on myself. From there, Katherine explored things I have wanted from my dad. My list included spending time with him, doing things I like with him, talking about emotional things, maintaining a bonded relationship, and feeling validated by him. Katherine explored my current relationship with my dad. She inquired how we currently function. We get upset but we make amends, he gives me things even if he can't afford it, for the most part he stays out of my life and leaves me feeling like a problem child. Having explored all these things, Katherine reminded me that I tend to be a "resentful person" and "I am selfish."

Katherine then drew a correlation between my relationship with my dad to my relationship with God. I explained that I view God as my provider, that he gets me out of jams and has great plans for my life. However, I struggle to have a real relationship with God. I said I feel cheated by God. He has given me so much and has called me to do His work, but then has left me to deal with the fallout of homosexuality alone. Summed up, I feel God has screwed me over. Katherine compared my relationship with my father to my relationship to God and pointed out the similarities.

We closed out our session by having me speak all of this out to God. In prayer, I explained my feelings to God and cried out for help and guidance. Then, Katherine laid hands on me and prayed. It was a good session. To be honest, though, I'm sick of talking about my dad. From my meetings with Jackie to this one with Katherine, I'm struggling to see the benefit. In fact, the more I talk about my relationship with my dad, the more confusing it becomes. I fear I'm beginning to say things that aren't even true.

———————◦———————

IT IS TELLING TO realize I could have been saying things about my parents that weren't true to keep up the appearance of "making progress," especially in discussing my father. Looking back, I'm a bit embarrassed at how easily I was convinced to disparage my relationship with him. While he *was* often emotionally distant, my dad has done so much for me. I honestly do not have words to describe how good of a dad he was, and I could not have asked for a better father. I had a lot to learn over the years. Just because someone isn't constantly emotionally available the way *you* would wish them to be, doesn't mean they aren't implicitly there for you. Having said that, the facility had a curriculum blaming the parent-child relationship—causing children to grow up to be gay, an over-enmeshed mother and emotionally distant father. They needed my narrative to match this assumption in order to satisfy the program's requirements for "progress."

NH needed a "reason" to explain *why* I was gay. Parents make for excellent scapegoats in all kinds of therapy (not just the Evangelical Christian variety). I probably should have told the staff I believed I was starting to fabricate trauma that may not have happened. I may *have* told the staff about this concern, but I can't clearly remember. I just recall feeling as though things seemed abstract and I didn't have clear answers. I was in an extremely vulnerable position and therefore susceptible to the staff's influence.

DAY 56

I was finally able to call home. Dad informed me that one of my family members talked with my mom, stating that she knew I wasn't at home, and I haven't been on Facebook since January first. She told my mom she knows something is up and requested an explanation. So, my mom told her I am in California for rehab. My dad called another member of my family and explained that this is a family secret. Grandma and Grandpa can know nothing of it. Interestingly, my parents did not share the actual reason I'm here. Now that the entire extended family (except my grandparents) knows I'm here to get help, my return home will inevitably be uncomfortable and awkward. I can already imagine what this person's look and attitude toward me will be like. Ugh ... I hate this situation!

As I EXPLAINED IN the introduction I had a very close and tight-knit extended family. Everyone knew everyone's business. Having said that, up until this point, my extended family did not know my reason for being in California. It was therefore not incredibly surprising when this family member asked my mother for details. My parents had intentionally kept that information close to their vests. I do not believe my parents kept this information from the family out of embarrassment, but rather out of protection for me. Further, it should be noted that this was a difficult experience for them as well as myself. My parents were concerned with my alcohol use, and they wanted me to get help for alcoholism without judgment from family or friends. Changing my same-sex attraction was not the only reason my parents had sought treatment for me.

DAY 58

At church, I was faced with the same dilemma as last week. I put my blinders on and focused on the female singer. I tried to muster feelings of attraction, but to no avail. I found her voice attractive but that was all. As soon as the male singer joined in, my attention was diverted. Does he really have to wear tight jeans and have his hair perfect? As I lost focus and attention on the female, I knew I'd lost the battle. But then it hit me! My goal doesn't have to be a complete change in how I view men. I can be attracted to them, yes, but I also have a say in taking that attraction further. I can just acknowledge it and let it be. I have been beating myself up for thinking a guy is attractive, but maybe that's the wrong perspective. My sin is not in finding him attractive. Acting on that attraction is what would be sinful. Granted, I still hit a roadblock with the whole "woman" thing. Small steps. Small steps.

<hr />

THE IDEA MAY SEEM foreign to people not involved with a religious institution, but the idea that, "It's okay to be attracted to men, as long as I don't act on it," is a stance commonly adhered to by Evangelical Christian leaders, organizations, and churches. A prime example is a popular U. S.-based organization called "Revoice". Their mission is "...*to support and encourage gay, lesbian, bisexual, and other same-sex attracted Christians—as well as those who love them—so that all in The Church might be empowered to live in gospel unity, while observing the historic Christian doctrine of marriage and sexuality...*"[1] Their premise (along with that of many other organizations/churches) essentially says, "It's 'okay to be gay' if one lives a life of celibacy, as that is what the 'historic Christian doctrine of marriage and sexuality' states."

Aside from changing one's sexual orientation, The Church's answer to homosexuality is, in a nutshell, *celibacy*. For some, this answer may seem like a source of hope—a commitment a gay individual can make to still be in "a right relationship with God." In my past I have tried to find some solace in anticipating and attempting a celibate life. However, I no longer adhere to anything close to this expectation for myself. Being alone for the rest of my life, for fear of some unknown "Hell" is not the type of life I want to live in the here and now.

When I signed up with NH I was hoping they would provide an intensive program, giving specific and *practical* guidance on what to do and what not to do in order to "recover" from homosexuality. Once there, being told I had to come up with all of my answers on my own, made me feel like the staff didn't really have the answers (or really, even know what they were doing). As a result, I was resistant to completing my assigned homework.

DAY 59

Christopher showed up after morning meditation and specifically asked to speak to me. While I enjoy speaking to Christopher, his private visits generally mean something is wrong. He shared Hebrews 12:1-2 with me.

"Therefore, since we are surrounded by so great a cloud of witnesses, let us also lay aside every weight, and sin which clings so closely, and let us run with endurance the race that is set before us, looking to Jesus, the Founder and Perfecter of our faith, who for the joy that was set before Him endured the cross, despising the shame, and is seated at the right hand of the throne of God."

Christopher then shared that he and Jackie had discussed my hesitation in "going under" during our last session. Christopher said he fears I am mentally checking out of treatment. He believes I still have work to do. He referenced the above scripture and stated he does not believe I have reached that point in my walk with Christ. I highly doubt I'll ever reach that point, but I do agree that work needs to be done. I did my best to assure Christopher that I am still very much in treatment and have not checked out.

Christopher encouraged me to ask staff and clients for feedback. He also offered to let me move down to the other house. If Christopher were to approve that move, I would be thrilled, but I believe Katherine is set on me staying right where I am. I advised him to speak to Katherine, but said I will be content no matter where I am.

———◆———

CHRISTOPHER CONFRONTED ME WITH an assumption that I was mentally checking out of treatment. What I feel I was *really* experiencing was exasperation and frustration with the "process." I wanted more practical applications out of NH's program than what I was receiving, and I was frustrated that things weren't moving more quickly. This was especially true since I didn't feel the support I needed was being provided. I honestly wanted to close my eyes and magically move time forward ninety days—in theory, I would then be straight and sober. I didn't care what NH would have to do to make these aspirations a reality, but this was the hope and desire behind me being in the program in the first place.

Knowing I had a meeting with Melissa, I immediately went to my room after the group and cranked out the home-work she'd assigned. I thought it was pretty good. I even had Gavin look over it. Melissa, on the other hand, didn't buy it so easily. She challenged me to go more in-depth in several sections including "healthy relationships", "support system", and "my relationship with God". She also did not find my codependency satisfactory for healthy relationships.

I made some new commitments with Melissa. I will not self-isolate. I will be more forgiving toward others and make compromises. I will strive to cut out an "all or nothing" mentality. I will be invested in people, and no longer use people to meet my needs. I will learn to trust others.

We assessed the kinds of people I have attempted befriending in the past. I realized I have always gravitated toward associating with people I have deemed solid, popular, important, and (in some cases) Godly. I have sought to receive validation through association with certain individuals. I do not need to do that anymore. Things have changed! After treatment, I will attend graduate school. There, I will seek to form friendships and common ground with people like me—people who are naturally compassionate, loving, caring, and outgoing. I won't have to try and be someone I am not, nor will I have to work to prove myself. It's a crazy thought!

Melissa read over my planned 'support system' but asked me where I was going to meet people to fulfill these roles?" I said I hope to meet them through church. Melissa asked, "How prevalent are 'in-the-closet' gays in The Church?" Without even thinking of where she might be going, I stated closeted gays are very prevalent in churches. I discussed how uncommon it is to not have at least one closeted gay in any given church, with the kicker being the leaders and congregation often have no idea! Melissa caught me by saying "What will you do when you find yourself befriending an 'in-the-closet' gay in your church." I could feasibly engage in an ungodly relationship without anyone knowing. So, what would I do then? The answer was obviously accountability.

Lastly, Melissa challenged what I had written about God. I described my past with God but had given no practical plan to maintain that relationship. Normal Christian responses worked here. "Daily Scripture. Church. Bible Study. Friends who follow Christ." Nothing new here, I just hadn't been very thorough.

To close the session, Melissa went into a predestination spiel, assuring me that all that has happened to me has been no surprise to God. My future has already been written. All

I must decide, is who to choose: God or my flesh? While I desperately wanted to object to this, I kept my mouth shut. She ended the session with this: "All you need to do is be truthful and honest with God. God will take care of the rest."

I left her office, unsure of what I was feeling. Was it good or bad? I was frazzled by her take on predestination, but the rest was encouraging. In fact, I was able to flesh something out, which has added clarity to my situation. I consider such clarity a positive outcome.

As a now-licensed clinical social worker, I have some serious issues with addressing predestination in a therapy session. This is a perfect example of what distinguishes therapy done under a religious institution with religious motivations from therapy accredited by an academic institution. I understand that Melissa mentioned predestination as an attempt to be encouraging, but it was blackened by the all-too-familiar choice, "God or my flesh?" It was encouraging to a degree. In the end, however, this placed guilt and responsibility back onto me, further perpetuating guilt and shame if my attempts to end same-sex attraction weren't resolved. This was purely unethical.

DAY 60

Christopher set the stage this morning. He called on the phone to talk to me. He asked if God had revealed anything to me since my conversation with him yesterday. I didn't want to say no, so I told him I'm doing what I can, and hoping God will show up. He stated that Katherine expressed some concern in telling me what I should work on. He believes God will reveal what I should work on in the next week or so, and my goals will likely become evident when I see my parents this weekend. He implied my fears about "going under" with Jackie are too great and I may want to explore alternative means of addressing my pain. I appreciated the suggestion, but I honestly don't believe there is any more pain to explore. Christopher told me he was praying for me, and we ended the call.

I CAN'T SAY ENOUGH about the uniqueness of the Katherine-Christopher duo. Christopher believed his connection to the Holy Spirit was uniquely strong. He used this "connection" to guide his decisions and actions. I believe it was from this place of certainty he spoke with such confidence in the assumption that he knew God's plan for my life.

During an Experiencing God lesson, a verse caught my eye:

"Whoever is of God hears the words of God. The reason why you do not hear them is that you are not of God." — John 8:47

Since I'm struggling to hear from God, does this mean I do not belong to God? Do I really have a relationship with God or am I just playing a game, going through the motions? Gavin discussed a list of reasons we might not hear from God, including disobedience, unforgiveness, lack of faith, unrepented sin, praying incorrectly, rejecting the Word of God, not waiting for God's timing, and not listening. A few of these reasons might be part of my problem. I have been disobedient in the past, but I am working to be obedient now. Not praying correctly could be part of it. I tend to only ask things of God. God's timing is always a possibility. The most likely, though, is probably my failure in listening for God to respond. I am going to need to work on this. After class, I began praying for God to reveal areas I need to work on, and what I should change. For the rest of the day, I kept my eyes and ears open.

I'm assuming that by day sixty, you've likely picked up on the fact that I'm the type of guy that is hard on himself. In this program, I needed explanations for why I felt the way I did—the reasons I struggled with what I did. If there weren't easy answers, I was happily sacrificing myself, taking the blame when it provided clarity or explained things away. I preferred to take the blame and sacrifice my self-worth. It kept things straightforward to be the one at fault. I think my resulting self-perspective wasn't accurate. I placed undue blame and responsibility on myself for the troubles in my life because it was easier to address than the alternative. The alternative being that there were things that had happened and were continuing to happen that simply were *not okay*. Recognizing this would have meant changes needed to take place outside myself, and I wasn't equipped to navigate making those changes.

I have viewed myself as a victim for far too long. My victim mentality has led to codependency. I've been co-dependent because I haven't taken responsibility. No longer! I take responsibility for my life. I am not a victim. I am a man that must face the consequences of my past sin. I have no reason to be codependent!

There is a pervasive message within conservative Christianity that says individuals who struggle with same-sex attraction are somehow broken and in need of repair. Something about their past or present life isn't *right* and these individuals need to be "fixed." I can recall using those words during the intervention I had with my parents and my brother resulting in my stay at NH. "*I want to be fixed.*" However, over time I came to realize the feeling of "being broken" didn't match my life circumstances. Yes, I'd experienced a traumatic brain injury, and yes, I experienced same-sex attraction. But I hadn't been sexually abused (admittedly, I did question this for a while and concluded I was not). I was raised by loving parents who cared for me and ensured I grew up healthy.

The Church, other Christian organizations such as Campus Crusade, and NH, however, needed to believe and wanted *me* to believe that because I was attracted to men, there was something deeply wrong and broken within me. This was why Jackie and Melissa were working so hard to "find the pain in my past" when there actually was no such pain to be found. I can say with certainty that *I was not broken then, nor am I broken now.* The sense of brokenness I was experiencing prior to NH and at NH stemmed from a childhood and young-adulthood full of indoctrination, as well as a lack of understanding and support from people around me. It was not based on some psychologically buried, and tragic life circumstance from my past.

Shame and guilt breed in isolation when fostered and fueled by religious restrictions and dogma. To put it more simply, I was conflicted because The Church I loved, and to which I had invested so much time, heart, and sacrifice, claimed to know what was "right" for me and my sexuality. However, my heart and mind were telling me The Church was in fact, *wrong*. Looking back, what is sad is this constant and agonizing internal conflict didn't need to exist. I have learned my sexuality was not something I chose, nor was it imposed upon me. It *is* something I have the opportunity to *embrace*. Nothing traumatic must have happened for someone to be gay. Even when gay people have trauma in their past, it is not the trauma that makes them gay any more than trauma causes people to like pineapple on pizza, prefer red wine over white, or enjoy snowboarding more than skiing.

DAY 61

I finished my assignment for Melissa. I also created a list of things to discuss at Katherine's meeting tomorrow. I hope by having a list I don't come across as manipulative! I sure have no manipulative intent. I just have some things I'd like to talk about. I don't think that is out of line but who knows?

Matthew took me to see Melissa. I read through my scriptural application with her. As I read it out loud, I was surprised with the confidence and certainty with which I had written. By the end, I was actually excited to go and apply all of this to my real life. It's weird how I am looking forward to living my life for God and remaining sober from both alcohol and sex. Now, that's a change!

I shared Katherine's infamous "list" including things I need to change with her. We processed each item. I have discovered that my analytical mind tends to explain my thought process in interactions because I want people to know where I am coming from. Interestingly, what I intend to be helpful is actually perceived as manipulative by staff. I need to ask questions instead of explaining why I am asking it. I'm not going to lie, that is going to be tough, and it goes against the nature of who I am.

Having said that, I realize how my efforts to be genuine can be incorrectly interpreted. If I ever want to get out of here, this tendency has to go. Regarding control, I just need to keep my mouth shut and mind my own business. I read my conclusions from yesterday about victimization and Melissa didn't see a need for further discussion. Finally, we covered the topic of submission. Melissa is like me and is unsure of what the staff is looking for and expecting. It was so good to be able to process all of that with someone. Melissa encouraged me to find scriptural support for each change expected, and specifically ask what tangible changes the staff are hoping to see.

LOOKING BACK AT THIS now, I was very concerned with the staff's perceptions of me. I didn't want to come across as though I was leading meetings or demanding certain things from Katherine. I had this inherent fear that I could come across as manipulative. Part of this is a result of my own tender-natured spirit that often read into things. However, there was another aspect—the control NH exerted over my life and my mindset. Everything I said was either agreed with (pat on the back) or used to make me feel chastised (reprimand). I did not ever know how my words were going to be received. I felt trapped and was concerned about what I should and should not say. I was therefore overly sensitive to how my words might be perceived.

Melissa ended up sharing a personal story. She described the life of a young man who got involved in The Church but secretly lived a double life, struggling with homosexuality. This man played it all very well, even to the point of getting engaged to his girlfriend. Then, the man got very sick and was diagnosed with AIDS. However, due to fear, he did not tell anyone. The young man began to die, and the truth came out. The man was unable to repent and died believing he was going to hell—his actions were beyond God's love to forgive him. Melissa looked me in the eyes and asked, "did he go to heaven or hell?" I responded that we can't know the answer to that question but that if he had a relationship with God then he went to heaven. Melissa nodded her head and then told me that it was a story about her brother.

She said she shared her story with me to illustrate how God is in control of everything. Where I am today is no surprise to God. In fact, God has my entire life figured out and all I need to do is choose Him. It's good to know God has a plan and that it's already written. In fact, it's a huge weight off of my shoulders.

I'd like to spend some time discussing my work with Melissa. Self-disclosure as a clinician is a tricky thing in the therapy world. Depending on the theoretical approach, a clinician discussing their own life experiences is typically either discouraged, or *very* delicately approached. While sharing her brother's story may have seemed convicting to me then, I view her decision to share as professionally unethical now. Her "story" had several implications including the following:

1) To be gay and a Christian meant living a double life.
2) To be gay meant being unable to remain loyal to a life partner.
3) To be gay one would have a much higher likelihood of dying of a serious illness such as Acquired Immunodeficiency Syndrome (AIDs.)

Melissa stated that she shared this story to "illustrate God's control and power." However, it really seemed more like a "cautionary tale" she told to instill fear and doubt within me. It felt like she was saying, *"Be straight or else this could happen to you!* Within the context of a therapeutic relationship, this is not ethical. That is why I had a problem with Melissa and specifically, this encounter.

Melissa did something I did not expect. She asked to terminate our sessions because she believed we had covered all that's needed. I have made massive progress and am ready to move forward. We reviewed all we had covered since my first session: 1) acknowledging sexual abuse, 2) recognizing it as in the past, 3) taking responsibility for future actions, 4) being able to express feelings, 5) combining feelings with NH's program to develop lifestyle changes, 6) creating a detailed plan of action, and lastly, 7) backing the plan with scriptural support. Melissa and I agreed I have done all this. I gave her a hug goodbye. I am going to miss meeting with her. I wonder if I can start meeting with Katherine twice a week now. That's highly unlikely but I sure would like it.

Melissa wasn't on the same page as the staff at NH regarding "*submission.*" However, was it best practice to end sessions with a client without first adequately answering all the client's questions and concerns? No. If a client is concerned about how a program is running, and the therapist is being paid by that program, it is common sense that the therapist should work to find an answer to ease their client's concerns. Not only did Melissa *not* have a clear answer of what "submission" looked like, she couldn't even discern what NH's expectations were for me. Then, she suddenly stopped sessions completely! I don't understand this reasoning. Termination felt premature, and not in my best interest. It became obvious, after this meeting, that Melissa was more interested in meeting NH's expectations and potentially her own needs than meeting *my* needs. This was the opposite of client-centered care.

Before we knew it, we were leaving for Wednesday night Bible study at Calvary. I actually wanted to go to Calvary tonight. I sat at the back of The Church like usual, but it wasn't because I didn't want to be there. I wanted to process.

Gavin joined me in the back row, but as soon as the sermon began, he dipped out to talk on his phone in the van. He was in the van the entire time. Even before we had left for church, I had a feeling something was up. In fact, I think there has been something going on for the last few weeks.

His being on edge all the time and so easily triggered/pissed off gave me the sense that he was going through something big. I haven't said anything because, frankly, it's none of my business. We may have major disagreements, but I love Gavin. He is a good guy, and he loves the Lord. Seeing him this stressed out makes my heart break for him.

When we got home from church, we all snuck out to the kitchen, but Gavin did not. He huddled in the office (his isolation closet), but I would not let him hide. I asked if there was anything I could pray for. His response was "wisdom and discernment." Aware of the delicate nature of our friendship, I didn't ask for anything personal. Even if I had, though, Gavin wouldn't have shared anything. I hope everything turns out alright.

Gavin was clearly struggling with something he was unwilling to share with the residents at this time. Based on his enigmatic and secretive behavior alone, however, I suspected Gavin had gone and done something he regretted and couldn't talk about. It was apparent Gavin was heavily weighing the impending consequences.

DAY 62

Working through my homework, Katherine asked about my roommates back at college. We explored the issues I had with them, focusing on specific details for each person. We concluded that I desperately wanted their approval and friendship for sexual reasons. They were older, popular, good with girls, partied often, good looking, fellow social work majors, athletic and had cool stuff. These characteristics were all aspects I craved and wanted for myself. Thus, I sought to do everything to earn my roommates' approval. In doing this, I fell apart. The primary problem was that they wanted me to accept myself (i.e., be gay) but I was a chameleon and changed depending on who I was around. Further, the times I felt comfortable being my "gay self," I was never fully okay with it. Katherine challenged my thinking with this question, "What business does light have with darkness?"

DURING MY CONVERSATION WITH Katherine, it was concluded that I had experienced sexual attraction toward my college roommates. This had not been true, but it did strike a chord with me. My college roommates were people I'd looked up to for reasons I'd mentioned, including they were older, popular, good looking, social workers, athletic, etc.

They were, in essence, the kind of guys I wanted to emulate. However, Katherine tied this admiration to my sexual orientation, which I do not believe was fair nor correct. I did not have sexual feelings for these men. Having said that, I do remember going along with Katherine's line of thinking because it made logical sense. As I have stated before, I was looking for a solution, and was willing to entertain anything and everything I was told by the NH staff.

> *Since Christopher came over for Gavin's resignation, he stayed and showed us a video of a play called "Hell Night" which was filmed in Kansas City. I didn't get to watch all of it because Jackie came to talk with me. She is going to facilitate a meeting or two with my parents, so Jackie probed me for information. She believes my family's dynamic is a trigger for me and must change. Focus was given toward my mom's critical and negative attitude. We even did a role-play switching roles between my mom and "the ideal" mom. From talking to Jackie, I realized my parents' visit is going to be far more serious than I could have imagined. I am beginning to get nervous about it.*

> *When Jackie left, Christopher had us all pile up in the van. We drove to the house next to Sober Living where Gavin had been living. Gavin had already packed and left. He was spending the night at a hotel with his girlfriend, which sounds questionable to me! Christopher let us raid the house. Gavin had left a lot behind, and I was able to walk away with clothes, a water canteen, hand lotion, gum, mouth-wash, and a robe. What a day!*

My relationship with Jackie was complicated. On one hand, I really liked her. I believed in the work she was doing. On the other hand, I felt Jackie made a lot of sweeping assumptions about me, the gay community in general, and essentially, what it meant to be a Christian. As I have noted before, her ministry was controversial because it tied religious practices with clinical interventions. It became difficult to recognize what events resulted from the Lord's work and what was the therapy doing its job. Muddying the waters between the worlds of religion and therapy made these experiences confusing, and I began to lose trust in any perceived "outcomes" from my work with Jackie. It appeared she operated primarily from a place of sweeping assumption.

DAY 63

Groups with Katherine will be intense and challenging, which is what I want. Time with Christopher will mean leaving the facility more often and doing things. While I am going to miss Gavin, the atmosphere is going to change, and I think it will be for the better.

<hr>

BOTH THEN AND NOW there has been a consistent back and forth in my feelings toward NH. I genuinely respected Christopher and Katherine. I had this expectation that they would do something magical to "fix me." I can remember waiting each day for some big change occur—intrinsically hopeful the staff knew what they were doing. Miracles were bound to happen, right? It was what I'd signed up for, after all. Regarding substance use treatment, NH's program wasn't terrible (albeit a bit overly religious). However, in addressing my concerns with my sexuality, I now know that at best, NH's approach was seriously problematic. I believed in the program's intent to help me but struggled with the lack of intensity and practicality. What I expected to receive and what I did received in treatment were very different. Through it all, however, I tried to take a perspective of "What can I take away from this situation?" even when I wasn't at all benefitting from what I was being told. I used my journal as a way of processing everything—keeping myself grounded.

Today was tough though. My anxiety about meeting with my parents is through the roof. A cigarette would make me feel so much better. I've been so tempted to smoke but have resisted. I'm kind of proud of myself. Three days is a big deal for me.

Anticipating my parents' visit to the facility was rife with unknowns and was unchartered territory. I was experiencing a general sense of anxiety about the situation. I had flown out to California all by myself. I had been in the program this long without my parents being physically present. Within the walls of NH, I had opened-up, shared vulnerable things, felt I had experienced the Holy Spirit, and had been myself. I'd been doing this alone for sixty-three days. On one hand, I felt I needed to prove I'd undergone the changes I desperately wanted and needed. On the other hand, I was overwhelmed by the love and support my parents could provide. I can remember experiencing warm fuzzy feelings anticipating their arrival. I also wanted them to see the things that had been frustrating me about my experience at NH for themselves.

DAY 64

I sat in the office and watched as my mom and dad came to the door. It felt extremely weird. I was thrilled to see them but was unsure of how to act at the same time. It's strange seeing people you know and love in a place like this. I would have loved to run up, hug them and just be "me," but I must conform to the rules here. It was definitely different and uncomfortable.

Jack let them in, and they met me in the office. I immediately gave my mom a hug and my dad one as well. Jack told me to show them around the house, but we only made it to my room. My parents were impressed by how nice the place looked, including my room. When I failed to take our tour further than my room, Jack came and continued the tour for me. I followed. The four of us stood outside chatting until Katherine arrived. Quick introductions were made, chairs were grabbed, and we congregated into my room.

JUMPING UP AND HUGGING my parents would probably *not* have gone against NH rules. I may have been a bit dramatic in saying I wish I could have jumped up and hugged them. Expressing this, however, did speak to a general anxiety about presenting myself as calm and collected (and, to appear as though I truly had changed for the better)

> *I know Katherine's practice is generally focused on one-on-one sessions. I thought she might be able to change that up for a family counseling session. I was wrong. I found her "shushing" each of us at different times. Katherine was cutting no slack. The meeting was very emotionally charged but not much new stuff was discussed. Essentially, the meeting was simply the family history I had previously described to Katherine.*

I honestly do not recall Katherine shushing us. However, looking back it wouldn't really surprise me if that happened. What I think Katherine was doing was trying to control the session. As a therapist now, it's never appropriate to shush a client, but it is appropriate to set firm boundaries. It can be difficult to juggle three different people who all have different thoughts and opinions to share.

> *A few highlights that came out during the family session. My dad shared how my life has always deeply broken his heart. Since I couldn't be happy emotionally, my dad confessed that he "enabled" me by buying material gifts in hopes of making me feel better. (My mom interjected that they coddled me growing up). My dad shared that he has come to resent my phone calls/text messages over the last two years, as I never have anything positive to say. I was never made aware of this.*

> *My dad described himself as an emotional person, but someone who is unable to discuss his feelings. He shared that when I tried to verbalize my feelings or dialogue about something important, he would redirect the conversation by stating that the three most important things in life were: (1) work, (2) sex, and (3) sports—not necessarily in that order.*

I owned up to my past attempts and successes in manipulating my parents to get what I wanted. I described the pressure I felt to live up to their expectations. I also confessed my tendency toward avoiding responsibility. I have made excuses, blamed others for my pain, and lived however I saw fit. Stating all of this was very emotional. My dad would say something, and I would choke up. I believe my mom cried the most, but we all shed tears.

We ended our session. Katherine stressed that we should not talk about the things we discussed at this meeting until we were ready and felt the Holy Spirit guiding us to talk about it. Before closing, she said our next session will focus on the question of what to do next. I am looking forward to this, it will probably entail a plan for my departure and what I must do to be considered ready to go home.

Katherine let me loose to spend time with my parents. We were able to go out to eat and do as we like for a while. We went to eat at the Olive Garden. It was incredible to be outside of the facility and to eat at a public restaurant. I haven't had this kind of freedom in over two months. I was extremely grateful.

We went back to the house to meet Jackie. We began the session by describing our expectations and fears for the weekend. Jackie focused on me and had me speak to my dad in third person. It was awkward. I shared how I wanted an emotional father growing up. Since I didn't have one, I felt there was something wrong with me. I continued speaking in this manner for about ten minutes.

Jackie turned the conversation to my parents' marriage. I was sitting between my parents on the couch and had to sit there while my parents conversed. Jackie drew one of her famous illustrations. This one on the differences between

187

males and females. She explained that most families become dysfunctional when the father is unable to emotionally relate to his wife. In the case of my family, my dad turned to sports. This left my brother and I to fulfill my mom's emotional needs. Jackie came down rather hard on my dad and accused him of having a religious spirit. She used passages from the New Testament to describe the intricacies. I sat there and was reminded of how I felt when Jackie had done this with me about a month ago. During that conversation, I felt convicted. That was when I began re-evaluating my Christian walk. Things had come together in a profound way. It was like the floor had dropped out from under me. I wonder if my dad felt the same way.

Jackie discussed the roles of my brother and I within our family dynamic. She explained that the most powerful thing my parents could do for me, would be to restore their marriage so that it exemplifies Christ and his design. In a Godly marriage, the love of Christ will be revealed. Jackie stated that if this is accomplished, things will become more difficult for me. I will be forced to separate from them. I will be solely accountable to God and will no longer be able to use my family as an excuse. It is mandatory that I take responsibility for my life, future, and relationship with God.

To close, Jackie had us go around and share our thoughts. My dad shared something notable. When he and my mom used to talk privately about me, it was always "Seth's" issues and "Seth's" fault. "Now," he confessed, "It doesn't look like we were right. I see that both my sons' issues were, in large part, our fault."

We left the house and at my request, my parents took me to Chipotle! I love that place! Eating there reminded me of college, and I felt somewhat normal.

When my parents took me back to NH, we sat in the car outside the house and chatted for a good while. I shared how the residents are treated and talked about some of the drama that happens. My parents encouraged me, saying I only have a few weeks left and to just deal with it. They have a point. I only have two to four weeks left. I can last that long.

Looking back on this day, I remember feeling a sense of anticipation for what was going to happen—overwhelmed by being so vulnerable in revealing who I was. That was my big takeaway. I literally laid all of my cards down in front of Katherine, Jackie, and my parents. No more games. No more manipulation. Simply me. Or at least the version of me I believed I needed to be. Ironically, that wasn't the person I am now (interesting how that works). But I digress. I don't know if my parents learned anything "new" per-se; however, they were updated on what had been taking place in the program, what NH had been teaching me, and getting to experience their own interventions.

Reading this day a second time I can begin to see Katherine's agenda. As I've previously stated, the general explanation for homosexuality in ex-gay Christian circles is having an over-enmeshed mother, and emotionally distant father. Katherine's line of questioning, as well as her approach toward my parents revealed her true angle. Her approach really wasn't all that special compared to any other I'd experienced. This was a bit disappointing considering all the hope I'd placed in her.

DAY 65

Morning

When my parents came back this morning, I was happy to be in their presence. Church wouldn't start for a while, so we drove around town for a bit. I found my perspective and outlook of this part of Southern California was different when with my parents. I've always seen the area from inside a van with the perspective of "a client." I was always being watched, even while out and about, which made the area seem dark and depressing. Driving around with my parents, however, made me feel less like a prisoner, and felt more normal. The city seemed bright, vibrant, and exciting.

We went to The Gate Church. I sat with my parents on the right side of the sanctuary. I'd always felt judged by people there when I sat with the other clients. With my parents, I had the opportunity to worship God without that sense of condemnation. Worship kicked off powerfully. A young man went on stage and said God had spoken to him. He had all the men come forward. All the men were told to pray with another man nearby. Jackie grabbed my dad and dragged him over to me. Dad placed his hand on my shoulder but moved in for a full-on hug. While the sentiment is something I have craved, the experience felt awkward, maybe it'd be better to say that I felt uncomfortable.

While still hugging me, my dad squeezed me and began sobbing into my shoulder. I, of course, had tears pouring down my face as well. My dad whispered in my ear, "You got your asshole nature from me." I thought this was a weird thing to say at that moment, but it was comical. He has difficulty expressing his emotions, so he deserves a break. Jackie brought us together and had us pray to cast out Satan. As I held my weeping father in my hands, I can honestly say that I felt compassion and love for him.

The pastor's message was good as well. The sermon focused on discipline and the need for us as Christians to live a life of conviction backed on spiritual disciplines. After church, we ate at Farmer Bros. and processed the service. My mom commented that she loved it and was impressed by the pastor. My dad, still struggling to express anything emotional, jokingly made reference to The Church building. Eventually, however, he got serious and stated that he believed the worship and message was a divine appointment for him. My mom and I made eye contact and nodded in agreement.

Afternoon

Katherine arrived quite late for our next session. Knowing the hectic nature of her life, I was not surprised or disappointed in her tardiness.

The meeting we had yesterday involved a recognition of the dynamics in our family, and how those dynamics had created relational problems. The focus of today's meeting was how those dynamics should change. Katherine zeroed in on my mom's critical nature and explained how that had been passed down to her from her father. To battle this personality defect, Katherine challenged my mom to do an in-depth study of the "Fruits of the Spirit," and to spend time along with God examining how to implement those fruits in her life.

My dad found himself in the hot seat. It was clear Katherine had talked to Jackie about yesterday's session. Katherine reviewed my dad's selfishness and tendency toward avoiding emotional relationships. For my dad, this manifested in hating giving any time to people when he didn't feel like it. Growing up, this selfishness hurt both my brother and me. My dad always seemed absent and relationally inept. Katherine told my dad that this must change. This change will require my dad to recognize his priorities and sacrifice an idol or two.

Katherine also focused on me. She brought up the ways I previously manipulated my parents to get what I wanted. She called me out and told me this behavior was unacceptable. She also explained how boundaries need to be put in place between what I share, and how I communicate with my parents. Essentially, I am being cut off with strict boundaries being put in place. My life is going to be much different when I go home.

To close the session, Katherine set a plan. I had been hoping to leave soon, but Katherine was not in agreement. She said she had spoken to Jackie and that they both agree I am not ready to leave. I will be staying here another thirty days. Katherine explained that I've reached the last phase of my treatment. She described it as the "equipping stage". During the next thirty days, Katherine explained that I will be slowly given privileges to re-acclimate to life outside the facility. She also shared that I will probably be seeing her more often. The focus of our meetings may shift toward me leaving, and me sealing my exile from the homosexual lifestyle and community.

Just as Katherine finished, Jackie arrived. We didn't take a break between sessions but plowed on forward. Katherine gave a summary of our session.

Today's focus with Jackie, my parents, and I, was how we deal with and handle pain—both as individuals, and as a family. My dad deals with pain through sports, my mom through helping and comforting others, and I, through isolation. My dad described the pain when my brother came out as homosexual, and then again with me. He shared that the first experience was hard enough, but then after learning about me, he completely fell apart. I began crying upon hearing this and that distracted Jackie. She was going to do the "New Heart" thing with him but was unable to take my dad back to the emotional pain because of my distraction. Gosh darn it!

Jackie asked how my parents dealt with the pain from me coming out, and how they addressed it with me later that night. Mom explained that they did not discuss the pain and rejection with me. Instead, they took me out to eat in hopes of making me feel better. I was taught to buck up, stuff the pain, and pretend it didn't exist. Jackie explained that such inaction was not right. My parents had denied themselves the opportunity to exemplify Christ and walk with me in that pain. She explained that Christ experienced pain, and He wanted to share my pain with Him (name it and grow close to Him through it). By suppressing the pain, it became internalized, and later became a force of destruction in my life.

I brought up my parents' lack of sharing and not identifying with what was happening to me. I remember asking my dad to share some childhood stories back when I was in

*high school. My dad had blown me off and changed the
subject. Jackie expressed that such sharing could have built
a stronger relationship and may have lessened the load for
me at that time. During this meeting, my dad shared a
story from his past. In high school, he had his pants stripped
off of him, and kicked in the balls—on the bus—in front
of the most attractive girl at his school. Jackie did a short
New Hearts session with him, but I'm not sure if it left any
impression.*

*To close, Jackie reviewed all that we had learned. My dad
admitted that he has a lot to work on, and that he has
been unaware of how his behavior affected others. My mom
shared that she was unaware of all the ways she blocked my
pain and prevented me from growing up. I shared that this
session brought up a lot of pain still in my heart, of which I
had been largely unaware.*

*When Jackie left, my parents and I spent some time talking
outside. We discussed the changes that have occurred in my
life, as well as how the future may look. My mom said that
Washington University may be off the table due to finances.
This caused apprehension, because going to Washington
University is my dream.*

*I called Katherine and was given permission to eat sup-
per with my parents before they left. We tried Red Lobster
again and were able to get a seat. Supper was amazing, and
so was the conversation. My mom was thoroughly impressed
by the hearts, sacrifices, and willingness of the NH staff in
helping me. She encouraged me not to view the next thirty
days as a punishment but rather as a privilege. My dad
stressed that I should take advantage of my time here by
fully seeking God. I agreed and I think I will do just that.*

Evening

Returning to the house was awkward. I hugged my parents goodbye and walked back into the house. I love this place, but coming back from quality time with my parents just doesn't feel right. The tangible sense of freedom brought by the visit from my parents quickly vanished. I tried not to let that get me down, though. In fact, I entered the house in an extremely good mood.

As I walked into the kitchen, I quickly remembered my responsibility in creating the grocery list and assigning chores but had not been here to do it. Kevin had stepped in and covered my jobs in my absence. I gave him a hug for his service and thanked him.

I went to my room and decided to catch up on homework. Christopher is working tomorrow. The word on the street is that he has been known to check homework to make sure we're actually doing it. After the emotional rollercoaster of this weekend, I do not need any more to think or worry about. I worked on Experiencing God and my Discipleship lesson.

After I was done, I laid in bed replaying the weekend and assembling all the puzzle pieces of my life. A lot had been said, and a lot was revealed with my parents. While I think the weekend was important for my own development and ownership of my sin struggle, I think it was just as important for them.

I took a hot shower and spent time alone in my room. Thinking through this weekend has been good but I skipped over so much. I pray that while I don't remember a lot of what was said, I will be able to recall some of the more important things and apply them to my life.

———◦———

DURING OUR CONVERSATION WITH Jackie, I noted crying and how this distracted Jackie—preventing her from doing a "New Hearts" ministry intervention with my father. I want to be clear. Jackie never told me that I'd distracted her and never alluded to it in any way. The assertion that I'd distracted her was purely based on my interpretation of the situation.

I'm a perfectionist. As a result I always want to get the full story before making a conclusion. If I could record every single conversation I partake in I would. I would therefore know exactly what was said, as well as any contextual effects. I think having my parents at the treatment facility was a sacred time for the three of us. The visit was limited to two days, and much had to be accomplished within that period. It was a special time and I wanted to remember everything. Maybe, just maybe, my parents and I would uncover some truth or key that could set me free from my troubles. That was what kept me going, and why I have such a detailed account of everything that occurred during our time together.

DAY 66

Jackie came over for the third session with her in three days. Crazy! With my permission, she used the Cross-Country story my dad had shared yesterday. Jackie laid out Satan's scheme in my life.

It basically looked like this:

1. Wound (rejection)
2. Scheme (humiliation, shame, guilt)
3. Lie (I'm alone, I don't fit in, no one cares, I'm not good enough)
4. Behavior Change (isolation, withdrawal)
5. Flesh Pattern (flesh pattern)
6. Sexual Abuse (I matter, someone cares, I fit in)
7. Bondage (I'm gay, enter gay lifestyle)

Having my life described on the board in front of my room-mates here came with a strange feeling. As I looked at the diagram, I was amazed at just how true it all was. Satan had done a good job.

Jackie mentioned a few things of note. She said, "Until I discipline myself (my own flesh), I will be unable to operate and walk in the authority of Jesus Christ to overcome and battle the demonic powers influencing my life. Jackie gave a short template to deal with this pain and rejection: (1) fight

*against the lies, (2) forgive those who have hurt me, and (3)
accept the truth about my past. After our group, I spent most
of my time alone in my room. I'm not entirely sure what
I was feeling, but I wasn't feeling very positive about my
situation.*

—◆—

As a licensed clinical social worker I view the diagram/schematic
Jackie presented as very troubling. It is disturbing that people offer "clinical care" to homosexual individuals while holding to the belief that these
individuals' homosexuality results from spiritual bondage. It's honestly
frightening. They were doing this all in the name of Jesus Christ, which
makes this *even more* problematic. There is a fine line between treatment
and a church service. When you mix treatment and spirituality, the
ethical implications become an issue. This was essentially an instruction
manual into the paradigm of how they viewed my homosexual identity.

DAY 67

I felt God telling me that I have to quit running. He is asking for all of me with the promise to use me. There are still parts of me that refuse to die. I then found myself at Psalm 94: 8-13b, Psalm 139:7-10, and Psalm 139: 23-24. His message was crystal clear, but God was not done with me yet.

I found myself delving into Matthew 23, the chapter where Jesus warned about the Pharisees. God has been telling me running is futile and I will not win. He slammed me by letting me know that I had done the very thing he despises. I took heed of this rebuke and started a new study on Pharisaical Living. The lesson I'll present on Friday focuses on the hypocrisy of the Pharisees and the struggle we all have in not being hypocritical. God has nailed me down and it is time I listen and follow.

I THINK I FOCUSED on Pharisaical Living based on teaching from my previous church. I can remember the pastor specifically calling out the Pharisees—relating Jesus's teachings on the subject to the modern-day church. I saw myself reflected in these scriptures. What was most compelling was the mysterious "call to surrender." Even in scripture I couldn't find an explanation to what they meant, other than abstract terminology. It didn't apply on a practical on-the-ground level. However, for whatever reason, I found these assertions convicting and they further rooted my shame.

We arrived at our destination early, which allowed us to get good seats at a gathering known as the Grace Conference. We came to listen to Kelly Lohrke, the pastor out of Kansas City, KS that had hosted the Hell Night play that we had watched recently speak. Before he spoke, however, we had to endure the pre-service activities. A pastor, not Kelly, came forward and asked the congregation to all speak their heavenly language out loud. I speak in tongues, or at least I think I do. I believe that openly speaking in tongues in church is chastised in the Bible. I'm certain that it is for the pastor, at least. I therefore found it very hard to take anything away from the service, and entering worship was difficult.

While I stood there, two nearby guys caught my attention. The way they moved and interacted screamed they were homosexual. As I watched them, they gave each other looks, pats on the back and shoulder bumps. I have no desire to have a gay partner or even to be part of the lifestyle. However, I found it difficult to see this. I know that it is wrong, and I know it leads me down a path of self-destruction, but it still has a hold on me, and I'm still attracted to men.

By the time Kelly got to the pulpit to speak, I had pretty much checked out. I was in no mood to listen to a sermon, let alone one that would convict me. The guy was dynamic and knew how to work a room and provided numerous stories and illustrations. He touched on some meaningful points. He explained that we are God's currency in this world. God is less interested in blessing us and giving us what we want than he is in using us to speak truth and reach a lost world. The message was good.

While I was convicted and felt challenged to take a step forward, I couldn't get past the gay couple sitting nearby. I took my normal seat in the back on the way home. I put my headphones on and rode home depressed and discouraged. Marvin tried to cheer me up to no avail. I was pissed and I was going to stay that way.

Looking back, I have seriously got to get a hold of myself when I see happy gay people. This self-pity crap I put myself through is not okay. I need something to bank on and turn to in order to combat these temptations. I created that plan with Melissa. I should start kicking that into gear. I can see memorizing scripture in my near future.

———◇———

I feel I should expound on what led me to become so discouraged after seeing what I presumed was a gay couple at a Christian event. I can remember two distinct feelings—one of these feelings was jealousy and the other was envy. I was jealous that they were so open in their affection, yet freely worshiping God without any apparent sense of self-judgment or condemnation. If they were in fact gay, being openly physical in this environment was brave and courageous—a sign of strength and a witness to freedom. These are things I was jealous of. And then there was envy. I wanted to be like them. I wanted to switch places, if for only a moment – to not only feel the freedom to be myself but to have someone alongside me. It appeared that these two men were close friends, friendship being something I desperately craved in my own life. Lastly, I should be honest, these guys were also quite physically attractive. So, there was that.

DAY 68

Katherine asked to speak with me in the office. We reviewed the weekend with my parents. I've been at a loss for words about the whole thing. Some good had come from it, but some of the conversations were very awkward. I shared my happiness that my dad confirmed things I had discussed with Katherine in our meetings. She informed me that Stage 1 of my new freedoms will be laid out on Friday. My fingers are crossed! She encouraged me to begin preparing by praying for angelic protection when I go out alone.

CHRISTOPHER TOLD ME THAT God would be revealing his plan for the rest of my stay and life within a week. I received this news with a smile and found it encouraging. However, I had yet to hear anything specific. If anything, I felt God had been throwing me through the ringer without any answers and without any clarity. Katherine did mention a potential plan of her own, so that may have been what Christopher had been referencing. Either way, I think it's fair to say that I was waiting on Katherine and Christopher's plan, rather than Gods.

I shared that in these moments I struggle to fully trust in the Word of God. I don't speak truth into my life and use scripture to fight that battle. In a secure, secluded and safe place, I can be perfectly okay. In a Christian bubble, I convince myself I can live a straight life and I can memorize scripture and draw close to God. However, when I leave that bubble, I don't do so well. My mind rationalizes all the truth of God over my life, but then I tell myself that this isn't reality, it's just wishful thinking. I don't have enough faith and trust in God to face the battles in the real world.

Some aspects of this journey became irritating, and some of that irritation stemmed from the staff's lack of trust in how seriously I was taking the program. I don't want to talk down to or about anyone, but I took this program very, very seriously. Take the details within this journal for example! All the deep thinking I was doing, all the questions I asked myself and them, all the second guessing, all the sincerity and trust I placed in the staff—I was thoroughly invested. However, I wasn't treated like I was. Instead, I felt like my goals and intentions were constantly doubted. In fact, at times, it almost seemed that the staff didn't even think I *was* a Christian. Considering the emotional and spiritual investment I was placing in my life through the program, this was infuriating.

Later, in group, I shared that I firmly believe there is a calling in my life but am unsure of what that calling entails. All I can do is wait on God to reveal and set up His plan. I shared that I am trying to spend more time in prayer and enter into that "secret place" with God. Katherine then challenged me by asking about my thought life. I shared that my thought life is a problem. I struggle to control my mind, to prevent myself from having personal doubts about long-lasting change, and tendency to be inclined towards homosexuality. I discussed last night's experience. I wanted so badly to worship, but the gay couple sitting to our left deeply upset me and made me crave same-sex relationships. I have no desire to be in a gay relationship, but seeing those men made me crave it at the same time. The message was solid and powerful. I felt torn between staying seated or

*raising my hands, crying or rejoining the lifestyle and en-
gaging in a sexual encounter. I was at war within myself, I
could not submit and replace my thought pattern.*

I was willing to go along with NH's claims. I invested in it, believing that God would be doing something—something magical and
something I had never experienced before. Deep down I believed that
following through with what this program recommended would result
in not only my sobriety, but a true change in my sexual orientation.
This change was the exact reason I'd wanted to come to NH in the
first place. My struggles in accepting my same-sex attraction were deeply
rooted in shame and guilt initiated and perpetuated by The Church. I
believed that The Church, (i.e., NH's Christian ministry) could offer
a solution—more specifically, a program which claimed to *have* the
solution. I was therefore working under the impression that the staff
at NH believed I would magically transform while in their program.
Looking back on this now, I'm not so sure my trust was well-placed.
I don't know what the staff initially had planned, but I do know they
made promises—their primary assertion being that change was possible.
Further I knew that even though I was sometimes mildly resistant to
recommendations which didn't make sense, I *was* following through
with all advice and suggestions, not perceiving any substantial change.

DAY 69

Even though I met with her yesterday, Katherine came to meet with me again today. Two days in a row? Heck yes! I appreciated this time with her so much. Due to the busy weekend and subsequent busy week, I had been unable to do the lesson out of the Homosexuality Workbook. Instead, I had her look at the plan I created with Melissa. Like Melissa, Katherine's attention focused on healthy relationships, as well as my tendency toward codependency. She brought up wanting to visit my college town when I first get home. She created two lists: (1) my Christian friends and (2) Hunter, John, and George. My motive for these two lists is the same: I want to prove to these people that I've changed. Katherine remarked, "Oh really? How are the individuals in list #2 going to react to that?" She had a point. I spent about fifteen minutes trying to justify spending time with them, but instead of proving myself, I actually dug a hole.}

George and my roommates do not support the lifestyle change I'm attempting. Sure, they want me to be happy, but they believe that happiness will only be found in accepting my gayness. Explaining that with Christ I've changed, and I can live differently will not fly. After fighting this point with Katherine for a while, I gave in to the inevitable conclusion: I won't be spending the weekend in my college town when I leave.

That took the conversation to my hometown and the rejection I experienced there. Katherine seemed to be aiming to talk about rejection from my dad, but I brought up how much I disliked my hometown to distract her. I had talked about this with Jackie, but I guess I had never shared it all with Katherine. We began discussing my hometown with an analysis of my relationships with some of my peers from my class such as Brian, Jeremiah, and Aaron. These three guys were very popular in my class and guys I frequently tried to fit in with without much success. Having said that, Brian and I had a decent relationship through most of high school, but I never felt part of the "in" crowd. I wasn't also accepted by guys like Jeremiah and Aaron. In my opinion, Jeremiah, Brian, and Aaron seemed like the most athletic, intelligent, and popular guys in our class. I often tried to make myself acceptable to them but never felt fully accepted. Katherine stopped me and told me this was huge and couldn't believe I had failed to mention the rejection I had faced there. I shared with her the memory my dad had shared and how bad all of that felt.

I'm unsure of the segway, but I ended up sharing the pleasure I now experience with rejection. After dealing with so much of it, the sense of rejection has become a comfortable emotional state for me. In fact, I feel like this is partly why I want to spend time in my college town. I want to experience rejection, and I want to feel their disapproval. It somehow makes me feel that things are "normal". How sick is that?

Katherine explained that this cycle must die. She insisted that I work with her on the rejection I faced in high school. I explained my memory to her—my memories from high school are spotty, except the themes surrounding traumatic events. We took my memory problem to prayer, and begged God to break the walls preventing me from recalling memories. I honestly think there is some kind of barrier protecting me from something I'm not consciously aware of happening to me. Crazy, right? With that we ended our session. The rest of the day was extremely chill. We spent one group working on our Bible studies, which we'll present tomorrow morning.

———◦———

I WAS EXPECTED TO go with the assumption that the staff at NH knew what a good Christian looks like—that there are specific characteristics unique to individuals who profess to be "Christian." Anyone who doesn't embody these characteristics would just be acting or pretending to be "good" (and likely going to Hell and/or going to lead me astray). This was interesting to me. Even though Katherine, Christopher, Jackie, and other staff acted as though they knew the supposed "type of person" with whom I should be associating, the specifics in describing this person were vague and ambiguous. Figuring out what the staff wanted (both for myself and the people with whom I would associate), what to do, how to act, and who to befriend, was like trying to catch light at the end of the day or sand as it slides through your fingers—seemingly possible, but not grounded in reality. The staff stood in a place of spiritual authority above the residents, and this authority was never to be questioned. Conversations with Katherine, for example, were revealing in that she made authoritative recommendations and statements about my past and future friendships. She felt very comfortable telling me which friends were "better" for me—the obvious answer always being "Christians."

Besides the potential for substance use (which resided in either Christian or non-Christian groups alike), I wonder what other nefarious activities Katherine suspected I might partake in with any of my non-Christian friends? To assume my Christian friends were somehow safer and more wholesome was a bold assumption—not really based on any type of known fact. Quite honestly, it was judgmental as hell—judgmental toward me (having gone through this program) and judgmental toward anyone else I might come to know.

After the staff meeting and just before supper, Matthew called me into the office. I had put in a pass for my friend Davis to come see me. Katherine had called and I was approved for a visit, but he's busy this weekend. I get to call him tomorrow! In other news, my phone privileges will continue to be restricted. While this would have normally upset me a great deal, I don't care so much anymore. Matthew informed me that next week I am being given the privilege of taking a bus and riding to Target and back. Whoa. I really appreciate the thought and will enjoy it. There's a part of me that feels like I'm five years old and was just given permission to cross the street by myself. It's kind of humorous, but I'm still thankful!

I must admit I did stay quite busy in my own little world of thought while at the program. I stayed pretty wrapped up in my own treatment, focusing on what I felt was right vs. what I felt was wrong, keeping this detailed journal. My introversion and self-isolation often kept me out of other people's business. I'm therefore unsure whether the other residents had similar restrictions placed on them. However, it would not surprise me if it was just me most of the time. I hate to say that but that's how it felt.

DAY 70

When I returned to the house, Christopher let us watch "28 Days." I was shocked. I absolutely love this movie: it stars Sandra Bullock and Viggo Mortenson. It's about the life of Quinn (Sandra) and her experience in a rehab facility. I had seen it a few years back but wouldn't have dreamed I could watch it here. We aren't allowed to watch Thor because of its roots in Greek mythology, but we are allowed to watch 28 Days. 28 Days has plenty of curse words and a handful of sexual scenes. The rules here sometimes confuse me. Regardless, I was so happy that we were given the privilege of watching it.

I don't blame the movie for where my mind went, but after watching it, I found myself troubled. The movie accentuated the reality of why I am here. My life is going to have to drastically change when I return home. I am unsure of what my life will look like. On a practical level, some fundamental things will be different. (No drinking. No sex. No clubs. No partying. No gay friends. New friends. Accountability. Church community. And this list goes on and on). Sure, these things are daily practices here. They won't be when I'm living with my parents and then graduate school, though. How will I handle that freedom? I can't believe I'm saying this, but I'm scared to leave NH. Yeah, I fight things a lot, but this place has become comfortable. It's safe. The world I'll be returning to is not safe.

I'D LIKE TO SPEND a moment discussing some of the mixed messages I got from the staff. Most of the irony presented itself when Christopher was around. He often seemed led by the wind, changing rules on a whim. Most of the staff held very firmly to boundaries and stuck to the rules when it came to what we were exposed to. There were times we watched Christian films and sermons to keep us busy, but then randomly we were allowed to watch secular movies like "28 Days?" It was just strange. Being me, I was always trying to figure out the staff's logic. I think most people would not pay attention or care, but I was fascinated by it all and wanted to understand the reason for these discrepancies. There was a genuine curiosity as to why this back and forth occurred, but also an overall sense of irritation and a sense of lack of care.

I've discovered I have become used to a pattern—I've begun craving some form of rejection and have sought it out. Wait. I just said I'm craving rejection. That is weird. I'm surprised I wrote that. Well, this is my thought process: rejection has become a comfort to me, and I believe I did things in my past in order to receive it. It was intentional. I wanted it. I have got to get to the bottom of that before I leave.

All of the stuff I had discussed with Katherine yesterday came rushing to the surface. I isolated myself in my room and began creating a list of rejections I faced in my hometown. I firmly believe some of this memory recall came from the Holy Spirit. Thank God. My list is expanding, and I'll share later on when I am satisfied with the list. For now, I filled the front and backside of a notecard. It's amazing. With one memory comes another! I hope to get to the bottom of all of this!

I need to address my desire for rejection which was mentioned on this day. I believe that my desire for rejection was multi-faceted. For one, rejection was comfortable. I was used to it. I knew how to respond to and handle rejection, and it was therefore easy. On the other hand, I think my affinity for rejection stemmed from a deep sense of pride. Though it probably sounds weirdly twisted, through rejection I felt satisfied *being the best at being unworthy*. We all want to be the best at something, right?

DAY 71

We left to go to the A.A. conference. I was hoping we would only be there for a short period of time but oh how I was mistaken. I was not at all excited about going and was, in fact, dreading it. To counteract this attitude of mine, I did two things: 1) I had a conversation with a thirty-something aged guy over a cigarette. His name was Chris. Chris shared his life story with me and I'm not going to lie, it is a miracle he is sober today. I took a risk and shared my testimony, including my struggle with homosexuality. It was good to express it to someone I didn't know. 2) During lunch, I engaged in another conversation. We ate at Del Taco, which happens to be the most hole in the wall place I've ever eaten. As we ate, a man younger than me came in with a massive hiking bag. He used the bathroom and went back outside. It was clear that he had been hitchhiking.

After the main meeting, I ran into Joanne, who happened to be the NH off-site psychologist. Who knew? I had no idea that NH had an off-site psychologist. In conversation and due to her probing, I had mentioned that I'm here to change my sexuality. She paused mid-sentence. It was clear that she was not in favor of this. Joanne reminded me of the statistics pertaining to sexual orientation change efforts, stating that successful conversions are very rare and far between. I shared that I have my bachelors in social work and that I'm fully aware of the statistics. She told me that she'll be at the

*facility tomorrow and to end the conversation, shared that
there are many gay Christians in the world, and that she'll
pray for me.*

———◇———

Running into Joanne at the AA Conference was a mere coincidence. I honestly had no idea that NH had an off-site psychologist. That I hadn't yet met her seems obvious after learning information about what she thought of sexual orientation change. But wouldn't it have made more sense for me to meet with an off-site psychologist than a sexual assault counselor from a different agency? Clearly, the staff felt pressure to find a counselor who agreed with their ideology. I just find it interesting that their own psychologist didn't agree with what NH was doing. Looking back on what she said, Joanne was correct in her assessment. I wished I had taken heed.

*I have been avoiding writing about clients, but Robert has
almost hit my last nerve. Turns out, his brother was also at
the conference. Robert is as subtle as a two-dollar bill. He
would look at me, cover his mouth with paper, and whisper
stuff to his brother. At Del Taco, I commented on something,
and he smiled and raised his eyebrow to his brother. Really?
Really? Are we in elementary school? Robert walks an intentional five feet around me when he passes and makes a
point to stay as far away from me as he possibly can. That's
absolutely fine with me because I have no desire to befriend
him but is his childish behavior necessary? I'm considering
confronting him tomorrow, but I don't want to repeat my
experience with Ian. I'm honestly unsure of how to handle
the situation.*

Robert's behavior triggered feelings of animosity similar to the feelings I'd experienced with Ian. Looking back it is difficult to say whether his behavior was a result of actual homophobia or me being overly sensitive and reading into things. I should be transparent—I read into a lot of things. I still do to this day. I could have been incorrectly reading the signs. Regardless, Robert rubbed me wrong and on a fundamental level made me feel as though I was not "good enough."

I had spent all morning seeking God, and then I was thrown into the lion's den (well, it was truly barely anything but hey—I'm dramatic—deal with it). My codependent tendencies had been shot through the roof, and I became a true pain in the ass. Seriously. I was in a terrible mood most of the time we were there. The truth of the matter is that I chose to act, be, and continue in it.

This brings me to a very crucial question: how the hell am I going to stay committed to purity when my real enemies come along? If my mood is being altered by a look from Christopher and a conversation with Joanne, then what is going to happen when George, my roommates and all my roommates come at me? The temptation/opposition I face here is miniscule to what I have coming my way in the future. I'm scared to know the truth and I know I can't trust myself. So.... What do I do with that?

The end-of-the-day processing hit home, and reality was beginning to sink in. The staff's original assertions and promises were not coming to fruition. I was *not* a changed man. I was *not* the heterosexual man I'd hoped to become. I was still a broken kid, and still confused about my sexuality (though I did have an extra helping of guilt and shame to further explain it away now). This was the reality I was beginning to comprehend, and it was part of why I was starting to grow more comfortable at NH. The real world was *not* going to be "safe" for me. Back home, temptations would be everywhere. I had not been given any training in resisting temptation outside the NH bubble whatsoever. I'd only barely begun to buy into the ever-present narrative saying, "I was gay because bad parents, blah blah blah." NH had come nowhere close to helping me find realistic and practical strategies to address any future same-sex attractions. Fear about my future outside was starting to bubble to the surface.

DAY 73

As I finished up my chore, Matthew approached me and informed me I could go with him to get food. I jumped at this opportunity. I've only gone with him once before, but I loved it. I quickly grabbed my stuff, and we headed out the door.

Matthew has been having a tough week. His car broke down and was assessed to be beyond repair. Like any person would, Matthew has been upset with this turn of events. We picked up the food, ran it to Christopher and Katherine's house, took it to Sober Living and then took what was left to The Gate Church. (While at their house, Katherine had me come in for a talk. She shared that I would be able to use my computer during my free time, but that it is not to take the place of the time I would normally spend with the Lord).

Later on, I could sense Matthew's mood getting worse. His phone was malfunctioning, so we went to the phone store. The employee at the store was extremely rude, so we quickly left. Knowing that this was not helping Matthew's mood, I gave him a pat on the back. He told me not to "patronize" him and he preferred to be left alone. I completely understand this as I tend to be the same way. Luckily, the next Boost place was able to help him. Instead of having the malfunctioning phone fixed, he switched back to his old phone. While they did this, we ran by a convenience store to

*buy gas. I bought him a Monster to cheer him up. When we
arrived back at the store, Matthew had a cigarette with me.
I couldn't believe my eyes. I felt bad that he was returning to
a bad habit, but it was also nice to have a smoke with him.*

*After all of that, Matthew drove me to the Post Office where
I picked up my computer! It had arrived on Saturday but
since we had been at the A.A. convention, no one was home to
receive it. Materialism is bad but having my own computer
with me brightened my mood.*

*I have some thoughts to process. Spending time outside the
facility is so good for me. Watching people today helped me
see something I hadn't realized. Being in the house all the
time has skewed my perspective. Little things, like Robert's
comment on Saturday become such massive ordeals, when
in reality, who cares? I have been taking such small things
and turning them into full-blown problems. I've found it's
hard to see this reality when all my time is spent at the
facility. I'm focused only on myself. Having spent time with
Matthew, even when he has been having a bad day, I have
been able to rethink my perspective on why I'm at NH, the
goals I'm striving for, and the areas I should be working on.
Getting outside this morning was like a breath of fresh air.*

HAVING MATTHEW OPEN UP to me felt like a reward. He'd never really
been vulnerable in expressing his true feelings this way. Being alone with
him outside the facility was a cherished moment. I was mildly disappointed that my pat on his back hadn't been well-received, but in the
end I can understand why. Venturing out, doing errands, and connecting
with Matthew allowed me to open my eyes and see life beyond NH's four
walls. I felt like I was part of something. I was being regarded as someone
important. This may have been what caused me to begin consciously

processing life outside of the facility. Either way, my time with Matthew was important because it brought back some very significant themes deserving of serious thought.

Jackie came tonight and had me play Misty Edwards music on my computer. She had the entire group enter worship and seek communion with God. Everyone seemed to be connecting, but I could not go there. When I searched my heart, I came to a startling condition: unbelief. There are still things inside me that doubt whether God will deliver me from homosexual attraction. My conversation in my previous meeting with Katherine came flashing back. I can believe in God and his manifestation in my life in my current little bubble, but can I really trust God in the real world? Not only that, but can I trust myself? When opportunities arise and the temptation to act out with another homosexual male is dangled before my eyes, what will I decide? I feel like I'm standing on the crest of a slippery slope. I can fight and maintain my balance for a good period of time, but after a while, a simple breeze or gust of air could send me sliding down into sin and everything I've been fighting against. It's this uncertainty and fear, which I believe, kept me from going deep with the Lord tonight.

A couple weeks back I'd tried to comfort myself with the argument of celibacy as a potential solution. However, truth be told I was not satisfied with this potential future even then. I mean sure, I could try to convince myself that celibacy was a viable option, but it really wasn't and still isn't. I think I even knew that then. It may have been the ideal Christian solution and I may have tried to see celibacy as a possibility a few weeks back. In this entry however, I was arguing the same-sex attraction issue again. In my heart of hearts, I needed my homosexual attraction to be eliminated completely if I were going to live a wholly heterosexual lifestyle. Therefore, while I feel a change within myself would be needed to live in absolute celibacy, many celibate individuals manage to never act on inherent same-sex impulses.

DAY 74

Morning meditation got me thinking. Everything we do has consequences. The temptations I give into are not just moral failures, but with each encounter come specific consequences. I had not taken this into consideration when I was in college. I believed that as long as the people I wanted to impress, and the people I felt really 'mattered,' did not know about my sexual lifestyle, alcohol consumption, or the occasional joint, everything would be fine. I thought as long as I played my cards right, I could do whatever I wanted when I wasn't around them. I could not have been more wrong. I hadn't analyzed the consequences of my secret life. These consequences included the loss of integrity, loss of character and a change in life perspective. The changes were slow and thus, I was never fully aware they were taking place. However, what I couldn't see is that the people who mattered could see very clearly. As I slipped away, my denial prevented me from hearing the truth until it was too late, and I needed 'professional' help.

I MADE A STATEMENT saying the consequences of my homosexuality were not able to be kept secret. That was not entirely true. The truth was that I *did* play a fairly decent heterosexual. Most people didn't catch on to the reality that I was gay until I told them (take my own parents and Campus Crusade colleagues into consideration for example). What I meant to illustrate in this paragraph was that due to my behavior of acting out on my desires (including use of substances and homosexual activity), I was destroying my integrity. Whether people knew about it from the outset, internally I knew it, and the weight of the resulting guilt was enough to seek treatment.

As we arrived at Venice Beach, I could not believe my eyes. I had never seen anything like this. Palm trees lined the Boardwalk. The ocean was to our right, and a sea of culture in front. Marijuana dispensaries and licensed marijuana doctors had offices on every single block. Hippies were hanging out in groups on grassy areas, openly smoking weed. Street vendors were selling everything from custom-made glass to photography and handmade art. Homeless people were interspersed throughout, many were sleeping on the ground. In fact, we passed an unconscious homeless individual who had passed out. A police officer placed a ticket on his jacket as we walked past. Drunk people were everywhere, most of them had passed out the night before. In the midst of all this, was a thriving culture of tourists, locals riding their bikes, teenagers hanging out in groups, and police monitoring the streets. All of this was taking place on a mundane Tuesday at 2:00 in the afternoon. Welcome to California!

Amidst all this culture was a congregation of gay people. To the untrained eye, it might have been difficult to spot. I am not so naive. I didn't say anything to anyone in our group, but I was struggling inside. As I watched these men, sitting in the grass, holding hands and laughing, I began to want to be with them as well. I suddenly began experiencing self-pity. I wanted that kind of life and was pissed that I couldn't have it too. It didn't seem fair. (Note: In saying this, I don't mean that I want a relationship with a man. I have ruled that out and have no spiritual desire for it. My flesh, on the other hand, deeply craves it). To make matters worse, four young men were standing in front of me outside a store with their shirts off. My eyes failed me, and I found myself craving sexual pleasure, to just run my hand across his chest and for him to move forward placing his hands over my shoulders. Ugh... I digress.

What is the deal? This morning I felt regret for not acknowledging the consequences of satisfying my homosexual inclinations and pursuing that kind of lifestyle. I had felt genuine regret and did not want to do it all over again. But then, less than ten hours later, I'm back to craving a homosexual experience and I find myself lusting after four men. This is unbelievably difficult. I've committed to living differently, but my flesh desperately longs for homosexual interactions and sexual pleasure. How do I overcome this insatiable drive within me? How do I stop myself from giving in? The pull and temptation are so incredibly strong. It attacks my intellect, emotions, sexual desires, and need for acceptance. All my defenses are hit.

It is important that I bring up the topic of healthy sexuality *regardless* of sexual orientation. You don't have to agree, but I now believe in healthy homosexuality. Any level of healthiness or unhealthiness can exist in *any* sexual relationship. As a compassionate human being, but especially as a social worker, I accept everyone I encounter for who they are. I believe that within each of us, people inherently *can* be healthy. There are many individuals within the LGBTQIA+ community who live completely conventional lives—lives devoid of substance use, not sexually acting out, and not even experiencing religious trauma. During the time I wrote this journal, I was clearly unaware (or maybe refused to believe) that mental and physical healthiness within the context of homosexuality could be a reality. Now that I see healthy homosexuality as a reality, I wonder if the other men in the NH program were battling with their own sexual temptations. There were many attractive women around (e.g., at Venice Beach). The fact that I was so focused on my internal struggle, without seeing my attractions as a natural and normal experience, is a struggle I deeply wish I could go back and uncomplicate for myself. Had I been able to accept myself for who I was, understanding regular human development and sexual attraction, I would have realized my behaviors were completely in line with healthy, normal human behavior.

DAY 75

*Of all the new off-site activities, I think I am the most
excited about going to The Gate. I am seriously stoked. I am
excited about venturing out. I hope to experience temptations so I can stand on God's truth and live out this new life
without giving in. I need to be tested in a safe environment.
That way, when I am tested in graduate school, I will have
practical means to stay pure and not be dragged back into
a hook-up culture. I know I haven't yet experienced the full
force of temptations and trials, but with the freedom I have
been given, I hope I will learn the self-control and conviction
to make it through without faltering. I think I am on the
right track.*

As I MENTIONED BEFORE, I was always bothered that we weren't allowed to attend The Gate Church more frequently. I believe the primary
reason was that it was Christopher and Katherine's home church. It
was apparent they didn't want residents from the program in regular
attendance. I got the sense something may have happened in the past
to give NH a bad for attendees at The Gate. However, in this entry
I expressed how thrilled I was to be able to go. The worship and the
messages were far more inspirational and felt more spiritually led than
the messages and worship at Calvary. Further, in being allowed to attend

The Gate, I was able to go alone with Christopher, Katherine, and their family. It felt like a special opportunity to not only grow close to God but also bond with Katherine.

The way Katherine presented this upcoming Saturday, it sounded like I will have an all-day off-site pass with my friend Davis. I am floored by this opportunity. If that actually happens, I am going to be unbelievably happy. Davis is one of the most committed and self-controlled Christians I know. Getting to spend time with him may be one of the biggest encouragements I have experienced being here. I pray he comes on Saturday. Hopefully, I will be able to call him on Friday.

The gentleman I was given permission to visit with was my friend Davis. Davis and I had become close friends through Campus Crusade back in college. Davis was a unique guy, taking spiritual warfare very seriously. He was a United States Marine. He therefore spent a lot of time overseas serving our country on active duty. The fact that Davis would be in the area and able to meet with me was a pretty big deal—not just from the facility's perspective but also from my own. I really respected Davis and looked up to him in a myriad of ways.

I know I discussed this in the introduction to this book, but growing up I didn't realize I was gay. This was primarily due to my religious upbringing and where I was raised. I was born and raised in an area of the U.S. with very little diversity then and now. Same-sex attraction and living a homosexual lifestyle were strictly viewed as sinful and perverted—experienced only by people of the most questionable moral character. Therefore, as an awkward, shy, church-going Christian teen, finding myself experiencing same-sex attraction caused me significant confusion. I wasn't a pervert. I was simply attracted to other males! The only places I knew to look for help were my Church and my high school spiritual mentor—both of whom pushed celibacy as the only option for me. The subject of homosexuality was fairly taboo, and rarely mentioned in my childhood. As a result, I was never really introduced to the concept growing up, and never knew much about it until I was experiencing same-sex attraction.

DAY 76

*Like most Thursdays, Bob came to lead our morning groups.
We had been discussing tools for our recovery from a list of
one hundred options. I picked the tool "Remember your last
drink" and began sharing. I was shocked and disappointed
in what I shared. From the stuff happening in the house,
the memories I recounted in my journals, to the fears of my
future departure, I completely backtracked. What I shared
was the same doubts, fears, and frustrations I had expressed
during my first week here. I was viewing my struggle in my
logical mind instead of trusting God and giving myself to
Him.*

*I vented for about ten to fifteen minutes that I feel I'll never
be happy, either gay or straight. If I'm gay I'll feel like I'm
going to hell, and if I'm straight I'll feel like I'm faking and
not being true to myself. I was right back at square one. I
couldn't believe I had just said all of that. To make it all
worse, Robert was smiling and laughing at me the whole
time. I didn't care, though.*

*After the group I asked Marvin to come outside for a smoke.
I asked for his honest opinion about what had just happened. Before he began, I shared with him that I was extremely disappointed in myself—that I had no idea where
all that negativity came from. I thought I had moved past
it! Marvin shared that he thinks I haven't fully surren-*

226

dered and that I may still be looking for excuses to give in. I took these words to heart and thought seriously about them. Am I still holding back?

I went into the house and approached Bob. I apologized for my behavior and told him that it was out of character for me. I explained my nervousness toward leaving. In talking, I expressed that I truly regard my homosexual desires as an addiction. However, since most gay individuals regard these desires as a lifestyle, I find myself trapped and confused. I have no desire to be gay, and acting out is simply a way I learned to cope with loneliness and depression. As we continued to talk, I said something that surprised me. In the past, I have correlated sex with friendship. Beginning with my coworker at the fireworks stand around age fifteen, I ended up messing around with other friends. I equated love with sex. Perhaps, that is why I've never felt I had real friendships with Brian, Michael and Ethan. I had never desired to act out with them, but without having had a sexual encounter, I subconsciously wasn't satisfied. Knowing all this, how will I keep my reservations toward acting out when I'm in graduate school?

IN BOB'S GROUP, I was beginning to face the reality that I would soon be leaving the program. As I squared up with this truth, I was overwhelmed. I knew, deep down, that I had not changed and that if I was to be successful at sexual orientation change, more than mere proclamations and dedications would be required. *Change* was what had been promised when I started the program, but change was not what I experienced. That I was going to be leaving without any meaningful transformation began to fully sink in during this meeting. I was grappling with the fact that I wouldn't be able to successfully carry this change out, which would be completely *on me*—my shortcomings, my fault. My fears and worries about my capabilities were coming to the forefront. In a way, this was a "lightbulb moment," but my fears were met with further negativity and fear. I was realizing my sexuality wasn't a choice—my sexuality was something I *couldn't change.*

Katherine came and met with me at noon. I shared some key passages from my journals that my mother had sent me in the mail. She was happy that my mom had sent them to me. I also confessed my backslide in group, and that I couldn't believe I had gone back and said all of that. She encouraged me to catch myself and get myself back in alignment with God.

She stressed two passages in last week's homework. The passages communicated that once we make a commitment to the Lord, intimacy with Him increases and that once we are in a right relationship with him, He can use us as "instruments" to bring about healing to others. Katherine explained that this is what I've been doing since I came to NH. I first needed to get things right with God. Then, as I worked through my issues, I grew in my relationship with the staff and other clients. Through them, I've received acceptance and healing.

From there, we focused on my perceived need to prove myself to my classmates in my hometown. Having been rejected and neglected, I wanted so badly to stick it to them and prove I wasn't a loser, failure, reject, and loner. We explored an event from last Christmas, where I went to a local bar in hopes of proving myself. Instead of proving my success, I got drunk and isolated, and expressed rejection through the form of self-pity.

My hometown has instilled a sense of rejection in me. Rejection has become a comfort and identity. As a result, I seek it out. It's what I'm used to, and it feels right. My desire to prove myself is, in fact, proof of bondage to rejection. I enter situations already knowing the outcome but hoping it will go differently. I have this hope because I refuse to let go. Katherine shared that I will never live a whole life until I deal with the pain and let go. She said that dealing with pain is an essential thing I do with Jackie. In preparation for this meeting and to find lasting healing I must stand on the Word of God denouncing this identity and bondage. I must begin speaking the truth about my life and casting down the lies I believe.

In today's entry, I refer to the fact that I experienced a lot of rejections during my youth. The truth was, I had engaged in sexual encounters with several of my friends. In a way, these encounters resulted from typical adolescent sexual behavior, normal for many teens. But on a deeper subconscious level, I feel I was trying to earn approval through these encounters. By connecting sex with friendship, I was attempting to establish and secure my worth with my peers. Further, as I've previously stated, I wasn't aware what sexual orientation even was. As a result, my feelings about my sexuality were very confusing. During this day's entry, I further tried to make sense of rejections my peers in high school.

DAY 77

Walking up to the trailer for the Overcomers meeting, Matthew pulled me aside. He told me to sit next to him at the meeting because he had several questions to ask me. Matthew went over the little grocery list I had created and added a few things. He also pulled my cell phone out of his coat pocket and told me to give Davis another call at break. I was ecstatic about that.

During the break, I gave Davis a call. He answered. The only vehicle he has is his motorcycle. His motorcycle has a flat tire and tomorrow it's supposed to be cold, and it's supposed to rain. Davis stated that he had a friend who was willing to come and bring her car. So, he could potentially come, but he would be bringing a girl. He could only stay for a few hours because he had to be back in San Diego in the afternoon. I asked him to text Katherine and explain the situation because, with all the rules, I had serious doubts that she would be okay with a girl coming along. I stressed that he should text Katherine and ended the call.

This turn of events seriously impacted my outlook. I have been hoping for and looking forward to seeing Davis since day 1. I didn't see that there was any way in which Katherine would give the ok for an extra person coming along. Even if she did, Davis could only hang out for a couple of hours. I have been given a full day pass and now it would be reduced to two hours, if not completely canceled. The day I had been looking forward to for so long was suddenly not so hopeful.

I WANT TO TALK about my relationship with my friend from that time. Davis saw me experiencing some of the worst moments of my college career. I can remember being so depressed trying to meet "God's expectations" as taught by religious groups such as Campus Crusade, I realized I couldn't win. I threw in the towel, resorting to substance use to try and gain some relief from the ever-present guilt and shame. I remember Davis coming to visit me as I was completely plastered from alcohol. My inebriated state wasn't ever pretty. However, given that Davis had seen me and stuck by me despite those moments, I desperately wanted him to see me while I was "making improvements" in the program. When I learned that Katherine had provided consent for Davis's visit and I was now living at the new house, I was overwhelmed.

When Matthew got off work at 10:30, he stopped by. To my surprise, he let me know Katherine was okay with Davis coming with his friend. Matthew still had my phone and I called Davis to know the approximate time he would be here. He said that he'd be here around 11:00 am and not have to leave until 12:30 or 1.

This is all getting kind of weird. I am being given freedom and that is not something I've been accustomed to in this program. When I get approval for these kinds of activities, I am shocked. Somehow it just doesn't feel right. Don't get me wrong, I am so excited about it, but it's different when things like this happen. I get scared of doing anything wrong. It seems to be too good to be true.

While in the program, I'd felt very restricted and isolated. Every move and every action were monitored and needed to be approved by the staff. At times, it seemed I couldn't even go to the bathroom without consent. Over time, I learned to trust in the restrictions and my lack of freedom like a tightly wrapped security blanket. It became clear, over time, these restrictions were put in place for a couple reasons:

1) to protect me and because
2) the staff didn't trust me.

Given my state of mind at the time, I believed that the facility had my best interest at heart. I therefore trusted in their process. When my restrictions were reduced, it felt like I had no control—that I was at risk of a relapse. I had been trained to believe that the restrictions would equal protection, which would in turn ensure my safety. Reduce the restriction and then what? I had become too dependent on the safety net NH had provided. Once that safety net was removed, I no longer felt safe. This freedom felt weird. When I think about it now, how could this system have even worked? Was it a plan which could truly set someone up for success in the real world?

DAY 78

With my abundance of time, I went back to my house and took a quick shower. I changed into nicer clothes, since Davis would be coming to see me. I met Matthew outside and we headed over to the facility. I unloaded a printer from the van and then helped set it up in the office. I switched it out with a newer one. In the process, I had to get the house's Internet password to enter it into the printer. Without thinking about it, I grabbed my iPod out of my pocket and entered in the password. It was incredibly stupid of me. I mean, probably the dumbest thing I've done here. Having that Internet via my ipod wouldn't have made a difference since I've been using the open connection for email, which is completely against the rules. Matthew saw me do it and questioned me. Since Jack was in the room, I lied. I was scared to reveal I had email access in front of Jack because I could lose the few freedoms I had gained. Matthew couldn't believe how manipulative and deceitful I had been. When he left, Jack informed me that he had known about me using email for a long time. By lying, I had affronted Matthew. Jack let me call Matthew and I apologized. Matthew said he is going to pray over what to do. I was overwhelmed with guilt and fear.

———◇———

ABOUT THE IPOD INTERNET debacle, I'm struggling to remember the outcome and any resulting consequences. I do remember I continued to be able to have access to the internet for most of my stay. However, there was an expectation that I didn't engage. I say this because I can recall communicating with George via the "Words with Friends" game app as well as emailing and using Facebook Messenger to contact friends and family from time to time. Based on these recollections, I feel I can safely conclude that Matthew spent some praying and decided not to tell Katherine or Christopher. Towards the end of my stay, I do recall Jack made a comment saying he'd always known about it.

I sat on the couch thinking through all of this until Davis and his friend Veronica arrived at the facility. Jack had them come into the office, and he spoke privately to them. After that, he let me leave with them. On the way to the car, Veronica said that she just felt like she was making a prison visit, and Davis stated the talk was completely unnecessary. I can only imagine what Jack told them.

Since we didn't have much time, we went to Denny's for lunch. To begin, I gave a quick summary of the program—what being here has been like for me. Davis showed me pictures from his contract overseas. It was amazing to see pictures of his time spent working in orphanages, helping small children. He shared a few war stories. One really stuck out in my mind. Davis was sitting in a cemented room checking Facebook, when a car bomb about one block away detonated and destroyed the building next door. Davis shared that he is considering going on another contract, and that he is not worried about death. He believes God is in absolute control. If he were to die, it would be the Lord's will.

Up to this point, we had stayed fairly surface-level, but not for long! Davis practically quoted out of my Experiencing God workbook, saying I must quit asking God to bless my plans, but rather ask God where He is already working. I must seek God's will instead of trying to satisfy my own.

Davis made a side comment that he really enjoyed speaking with Katherine. He shared that through that conversation, he sensed that she is proud of me. She apparently told Davis that she isn't worried I'll do anything stupid, which is uncommon. She told Davis that I'm a good person.

Returning to his discussion of God's will and not fearing death, Davis shared some points from a sermon he had recently heard. The pastor said if God is all-powerful, knows all things, and wants the best for us, He will likely answer prayers that are for our betterment. Thus, I should begin praying for healing, and the strength to fight homosexuality, even when I don't feel like it. Basic, elementary stuff, but good stuff, nonetheless. Along this thinking, Davis expressed that I must not care what other people think because it prevents me from being myself and experiencing God's power. He stated he fears I may easily return to my well-designed cycle of self-pity and victim mentality. I shared how this cycle is something I have been working on. Davis said that sounds good, but I better not have a Facebook status implying anything different (In my past, I used to whine, complain, and be dramatic on Facebook in hopes of getting attention. Yes, it was childish and I'm ashamed of it). Since Veronica was there, we also discussed women—while my type of sin is not typical, a Godly woman shouldn't judge it as being any worse than any other sin. Also, with time, it will be important that I share my past with any potential women, but preferably, not on a first date.

The conversation had primarily been on me, so I tried to kick it back to Davis. He shared that Christianity is much more attractive and meaningful overseas than it is in the U.S.A. He stated that ministry is not competitive, and every single person is valued for what they bring to the table. No one compares one another. Davis feels that this mission field is too great to ignore. He also said he wants to get his master's but wants to be financially secure before that time. Therefore, he plans on going on another contract somewhere in the Middle East.

Regarding dating, Davis said a girl would just slow him down. He wants to give God all that he has. A girl would make that more difficult. Typical Davis. I decided to charge their meal to my dad since they had driven so far to see me. Instead of going back to the facility, I had them drive me to my house. They came in and checked it out for a few minutes. Veronica took some pictures of Davis and me. The time with him was awesome. I didn't care if I didn't get to spend the whole day with him, I was so excited just to chat for a couple hours. I needed that, and this visit has brightened up my entire life.

Davis stated that "A girl would just slow him down," which will likely sound odd to some people. Davis had always been an incredibly attractive guy who continually attracted women, being a US Marine and all. He had an incredible physique, and an infectious personality. These were some of the reasons why I enjoyed being in his presence so much. Having said that, Davis's dedication to Christ was of utmost importance to him. Therefore, it wasn't all that surprising that he would put his commitment to serving God before women. Davis was very committed to ministry and service, often taking on the role of sacrifice.

However, I do want to mention something I've noticed, reading through this many years later. It seemed that there was a bit of a contradiction in Davis's encouragements. As he exhorted that I be open to God's will, he simultaneously encouraged me to ask for God to fix my homosexuality. This exact contradiction was not the first time I'd heard it. and it had led to so much confusion in my life. What would Davis have said if I'd shared that I believed it *was* God's will that I am gay?

What did he think I'd been doing at NH all this time? So many people have just assumed that being gay was a choice I've made, not how I was created. Why Christians always have to take a position of *knowing* right vs. wrong, then imposing that view on others is beyond me. It seems, from a Christian perspective, that God accepting someone for being gay is inconceivable.

Jackie arrived for our meeting. I explained my plans to move back to the Midwest and live with my Aunt Kelly. Jackie liked this idea. She prayed on and off as we went. I read several entries out of both of my old journals. Jackie explored the dynamics between Brian, Jeremiah and Aaron and me. I think Jeremiah and I both wanted to be top dogs, so we were always in competition. Jeremiah won the battle and therefore felt justified in using me for comic relief. I read the infamous e-mail Brian had sent me, which I had then posted in my journal at age fifteen. After reading it, Jackie asked if I had a difficult personality. A difficult personality? What a nice way to say, "Were you hard to get along with?"! I conceded that no, I was not an easy person to be friends with. I think this is still true to this day.

During adolescence, I was judgmental, and viewed every-thing through a black and white lens. I had this notion that everything had to be perfect. I can remember thinking, "If Brian would only do this...," and "If Jeremiah would only be this..." I had this puzzle in my mind, and if I could just put the pieces together to solve the problem, everything would be wonderful. With Jackie, I began to view everything as my fault, and I began to discredit all the things I've worked two and a half months to uncover. I said this to Jackie, and she tried to explain that none of that is true. I'd developed my personality because of my circumstances. I had no other choice than what I had been given. Jackie explained her position, and I partly believe it, but I do struggle to accept that it wasn't my fault.

Jackie explained how she saw it: The way I was brought up was not good for me. Jackie believes that if my dad had dealt with his childhood pain and learned how to be relational, I wouldn't have turned out the way I did. She described this as a generational curse. She shared that she sees two people in me: the real Seth is sensitive, caring, and loving, while the false Seth is harsh, judgmental, and tries to make everything just right by manipulating circumstances. This false Seth has used religion to make sense of life and bring understanding to any given situation. The problem is that this religion is devoid of any love. That is the problem. Since I never received relational love from my dad growing up, I had to manufacture my own version of love. Since I don't know what true love is, I haven't been able to receive Christ's love, or to express it to others. I think this has all changed since I've been at NH.

To close the session, Jackie shared that she believes there is still more work to do. She said that she feels there is still something that needs to be broken off. If this "something" remains, Jackie believes there is a demonic presence waiting to take advantage, and leap onto me. Thus, I'll be meeting with her again tomorrow. Before leaving, she told me to create a list of things which make it difficult to be in a relationship with me. I agreed to the assignment.

In this entry, I discussed feeling the need to "perform" for Jackie. Perform may have been the wrong word. Looking back I believe I was trying to come to terms with the fact that I still hadn't changed. I felt like there was still an expectation that God would do *something* (since acceptance of my sexuality was obviously off the table as an option). Yes, my time at NH was running out, but I was still required to participate and engage in the program activities. Activities still included meetings with Katherine and Jackie, continuing our focus on my sexual orientation change. As long as I remained in NH's program, I would feel some pressure to perform under the assumption that God still had time to "fix" me.

DAY 79

Matthew came over this morning to let me know that Katherine would be taking me to church at The Gate. I felt honored to go to The Gate and even more honored to get a personal ride with Katherine and her three boys.

On the way to church, Katherine and I talked about my visit with Davis. I shared some of the things Davis talked about with me, and Katherine seemed impressed. She stated, "Davis is the real deal, isn't he?" Of course, I responded with a resounding, "Yes!" At church, I was allowed to sit by myself wherever I wanted. This was a big deal, since we were never allowed to do that before. No lie: I felt a little special. I loved the worship. The head pastor was not there, so a different guy spoke. This guy was not that impressive. I honestly got nothing from his message. However, I didn't really care, because I had gotten so much from the worship session.

One thing did bother me, though, which I have kept completely to myself. I noticed a young man, probably nineteen or twenty, sitting in front of me. I have seen him every time I've been to The Gate, but for the first time, I watched him. I couldn't believe my eyes. This kid moved and carried himself in a completely effeminate and gay manner. I was impressed with myself in that I had no feelings of lust toward him. He wasn't bad looking. If anything, I'm

239

just curious what his story is. I wonder if he has gotten to
the point of dealing with sexual identity, or if he is still
playing the part. I decided to leave it alone, and admitted
it is absolutely none of my business.

I SHOULD PROBABLY SPEAK to my realization that this one gentleman attending the church was most likely gay. I was able to do so because of a sort of superpower called *"gaydar."* Put simply, gay guys can sometimes "read" the sexual identity of other men. More specifically, gay men often have an innate gift in identifying other gay men. I don't know what causes this, or what really sets gay men apart from straight, but once a man is aware of his sexuality as a gay person, it becomes easier to see it in others.

It also should not be surprising that some people at church are gay. I realize that now, but it was always surprising to me then. With time, I've realized that a lot of people hide in the shadows at church because of fear or confusion regarding who they are. I don't want to shortchange or diminish people's faith, but I do think some people hide their sexuality in Church because they don't understand themselves (and they're seeking answers much like I was). Therefore, it's not abnormal, and we shouldn't be surprised when we find gay individuals within the walls of a Church.

Jackie arrived with a young girl who was staying with her.
Her name was Bree, and she stayed in the back bedroom
while I met with Jackie. I made Bree a cup of coffee in hopes
of making her feel at home. Jackie and I met in the living
room. We both prayed, and the session began!

We began the session by again reading through my jour-
nals from junior high. Jackie felt my perceived rejection
was in fact persecution for the gospel. I am aware that I
have struggled with a personality that hasn't been easy and

"fun-loving." However, I do think that some of my pain and rejection could have been because of my relationship and proclamation of Christ. I will admit this could be a possibility.

Next, Jackie made me read through a prayer of release from victimization. The prayer was extremely relevant to my life, as I have a tendency/history toward operating in a victim mentality. After working through this lengthy, four-page-long prayer, Jackie invited me to begin praying in the Spirit if I felt led to. I agreed and we began pacing the floor praying. Jackie came over to me and began leading me through breaking soul ties. I prayed to break ties with my peers from my hometown, sexual partners: George, the worship pastor from the mega church growing up, Justin, and all others, my mom and dad and my brother. After finishing these prayers, a wave of peace and relief came over me. I didn't know how to move. My identity seemed blank. It was super strange. Such a large weight had been lifted off me.

Looking back on all of this allowed me to attempt to make sense of it. I made a decisive turn away from my hometown—to not allow anyone or memory from that place to bring about fear. I think my past identity was erased, and my current identity is now completely in Christ. As a result, I no longer seek validation from others, and the opinion of others no longer digs at me. I can handle what other people think of me, and they do not influence me. I can do this because of who Christ is and what He has done for me. I take responsibility for my past and my life. I no longer point my finger at others and play the blame game. All ties have been broken and Satan has no hold on me. I am secure in Christ. Lord, help me to live this out! We ended with a prayer.

I've shared the story of this journey with others over subsequent years. Through my sharing, I've heard many differing opinions on what people thought of the individuals in the program. These opinions typically apply to Katherine and Jackie. People have mentioned that Jackie left a particularly bad impression on them. Many have said they feel like Jackie was more than a bit "wacky." For example, who really talks about soul ties with any seriousness? I feel like this type of "spiritualeze" pervades a very small and specific sector of the Christian community which tends to over-spiritualize all aspects of the faith. The only other time I can recall hearing about "soul ties" was during a church service in my hometown. This church was known for being extremely charismatic and was regarded as kind of "out there" by our community. It would be fair to say that Jackie likely came from a charismatic background, the practices of which might be viewed by some as a bit whacky. Having said that, I never spoke disrespectfully to her while at the program even when I disagreed with some of her methods.

DAY 80

Matthew took us to the normal stop to pick up food. When we arrived, Morris, a gentleman that works for The Church (and is Katherine's father), was already there and had already loaded up the truck. We took the food to Christopher's house and his housekeeper/maid for his ailing mother came out and picked food for Katherine. Seeing that I now live alone, I also picked a crate full of food for myself. I felt a little selfish, but I quickly got over it as the food was good. My refrigerator is now full and there is no way I will go hungry this week.

We then took some food to Sober Living, and the rest to the facility while Morris took most of the food to The Gate. When we arrived back at Sober Living, I grabbed my container of food and ran it to the house. It was my prized possession, and no one was going to mess with it!

I HAVE DEBATED TALKING about this, because I don't want to come across as judgmental. I don't want to accuse Katherine and Christopher of having questionable character. However, I have decided to address something here—I *do not* understand why a for-profit substance use treatment facility was receiving public assistance by way of food. Given

NH was a for-profit agency, this didn't make sense to me then, and doesn't now. Weren't they making enough money to make ends meet? With the continual influx of residents, how could they possibly not? Perhaps in running the Sober Living facility they were providing a public service, and therefore qualified for assistance. But still, the food was given to *me*—a for-profit, paying resident.

> *I called my dad. He had talked to Katherine this morning and had verified that I could be coming home on March 30ᵗʰ. While I am very excited about that, he did break some not all too-thrilling news. My Aunt Kelly is not entirely comfortable with me moving in with her. She doesn't want to be held responsible if I were to backslide while living with her. I could be a potential liability, and she isn't comfortable with that. I completely understand her position, and I don't blame her. In the past, I have been quite the handful. However, if I can't live with her, this means I will have to live in my dreaded hometown. I won't mind living with my parents, I look forward to that. But living and being in my hometown is a completely different matter. Where will I work? Who will I hang out with? What will I do to pass the time? Those are all the questions I must address when I leave.*

The word from my Aunt Kelly was quite a blow. Hearing that I could be a potential liability is a difficult thing for anyone to hear. However, given the amount of information Aunt Kelly knew about me, I honestly don't blame her. I was not upset with her then and am not now. She didn't know the extent of *everything* I was going through, and probably felt the risks of having me stay with her outweighed any potential benefits. I can only imagine how she would have felt, had I lived with her and had a relapse or faltered in some way (in which case she would have likely felt responsible). I would never want to put that on her. I love my Aunt Kelly way too much. While this was unfortunate given my plans at the time, I understood.

DAY 81

I was experiencing a rash, so Mike and I both scheduled appointments at a doctor's office. This facility did not accept my health insurance and so I used Mike's phone to call my dad. We decided to pay fifty dollars to be seen. I couldn't have been more disappointed. I've had a rash and body itch for over an entire year, which refuses to go away! The doctor wouldn't even look at the rash and told me it was my nerves. He recommended me to take Benadryl. My dad had just paid fifty bucks to be told to take an over-the-counter medication. It was the biggest waste of money ever!

———◇———

THE DOCTOR WAS LIKELY correct that I was stressed which was causing a rash. However, I wanted there to be more to it at the time. I wanted a more in-depth explanation for my problems than mere stress. Looking back at it now, I think it's fair to say that I was under a fair amount of stress, so his diagnosis makes sense.

I went to bed and laid in bed for about an hour journaling and praying. Sleep was calling my name, but I knew I had a lot to write. Before falling asleep, my mind was all over the place. I have become so thankful for NH and all the freedom

they have given me. NH has become like a family. I mean,
Christopher, Katherine, and Matthew have dedicated their
lives to helping people. Since being here, I have been practi-
cally adopted. I am unsure if they view it like that, but that
is how it feels—especially since I moved down to the other
house. They take time to get to know me and I, as a result,
have gotten to know them. They love me and want the best
for me—genuinely. I feel so special having been here.

Reading this paragraph is a bit triggering for me given how different it is from my perspective at the beginning of this journey. I spent most of my time at NH feeling as though I had no freedom. In this entry, however, I discussed thankfulness regarding the amount of freedom I had been given. I also made a remark about the amount of love I felt from the staff, when for most of the journal I had previously lamented the ways I had been treated—not regarded as equal given my sexual orientation. What caused the change? I think as I neared the end of my stay, I began to look at things "big picture," and was trying to take all I could from this program while I still had time. It's not like I was yet to lose my faith or give up on a sexual orientation change altogether. Rather, I wanted to get what good I could from the program and apply it to my life.

DAY 82

Katherine individually called Kevin and I into the office. She asked us to co-lead a group. This was no normal group. She asked us to put the new client Dave in the "hot seat," and to call him out on his behavior. She essentially wanted us to help him reach a point of surrender.

The group did not go as smoothly as I would have liked. Dave had an excuse for everything and refused to take responsibility. The whole ordeal was uncomfortable. We closed the group by laying hands on Dave, and we prayed that God would help him surrender. It was all very awkward.

———◆———

IT IS HARD TO remember any specific examples in confronting Dave. I do recall that Dave presented himself in a manner that did not match the typical NH model. Dave was not overly religious, often used profanity, and seemed openly homophobic. He wore his opinions about controversial issues on his sleeve and frequently said things that seemed intended to make others upset. All-in-all, Dave wasn't meeting the expected standards for NH residents. We were therefore asked to confront him in group.

Matthew led a short group to go over some rules in the house. It's about time the staff started to crack down! It was a little strange for me. I felt a part of the receiving end of the criticism. But then again, it had nothing to do with me. I will admit some things need to change. I personally feel things have been getting out of control in the house.

I mentioned that the house seemed out of control. I believe that I likely was referencing Dave's swearing and the impact it had on the atmosphere of the facility. Given that NH was a religious program there was an air about the place that allowed its residents to spend time thinking in quiet contemplation. With Dave's arrival there was a change in the atmosphere. For example, Dave and Kevin were found sunbathing outside without shirts on. That had been previously unheard of, especially with me living in the main house at the time. Given my attraction to men, it was no wonder I was moved down to the other house shortly thereafter.

Calvary was interesting tonight. The band shared that Satan had been hitting them today but that they were still going to give God the glory. The worship was phenomenal, but at the same time, you could feel spiritual warfare taking place. It was kind of freaky. The Church had the speaker give communion. He had unfortunately lost his notes, so the service was short.

In writing these reflections, I have frequently "gone live" on social media to read the long daily entries. I have often written my reflections in "real time." I've found this to be a therapeutic practice, as reading through the experiences from these days has been a very difficult process for me. There have been moments while live on camera, I've found myself laughing out loud from sheer disbelief or embarrassment in reading through these journals. The comments about spiritual warfare at Calvary Church drew a good, hearty laugh as I read this out loud. Spiritual Warfare is *such* an overused term in many Christian circles, and one I frequently encountered (and used myself) in my past. The entire premise encapsulates "good" vs. "evil," God vs. Satan, and the belief that Satan is at work to interfere in the work God is doing in the here and now. In writing this entry, I must have perceived that due to the "attacks" of the Devil on the worship team, God rained down his Holy Spirit which is what made the worship so impactful and meaningful that day.

DAY 83

I had my weekly meeting with Katherine. As usual, she asked about my emotional/spiritual state, having been given more freedom. I did my best to explain, but it really came down to a single word: confidence. Being down at the other house and being able to explore the town, I have been allowed to transition into my real self. Being in the program broke down my entire identity and took each piece, remaking it into the image of Christ. Now, I'm taking each of these pieces and reassembling myself. I am Seth. I may look the same, but I am a completely different person. The old has gone, and the new has come. The expansion of freedom is giving me the time and opportunity to walk and live in that new identity.

Katherine then brought up a topic I have been dreading. She shared that she believes alcohol, more than anything in my life, has the greatest likelihood to lead me back into the gay lifestyle. We discussed all the good that comes with freedom, especially that I will be back in school. She encouraged me to honestly seek God with that decision. She warned that for me, alcohol is a slippery slope which could take me exactly where I don't want to go.

We switched gears and began discussing what my future interactions will be like with the gay community. She primarily focused on the fact that my gay friends will not approve of the changes in my life and will most likely emotionally and verbally attack me. She shared that when this occurs, I have an opportunity to love them, and show there is a different way. No matter what they say, I should be calm, non-confrontational, express concern, seriously care for them, and be genuine about it all. I need to provide and ensure a safe environment and show them love. All of that is a tall order, but since I have been exactly where they are, I should show them grace. Like me, they will need to hear about the hope Christ provides.

I FIND IT INTERESTING that I became more open and receptive once I was given additional freedom and responsibility toward the end of my stay at NH. I think this may have been revealing to the type of person I am and where I was then in my emotional state. I think having restrictions and being at the main house for a while at the beginning was appropriate. However, I think if I had moved down to the other house after the first month, I would have had a totally different perspective toward the program. I think part of my problem, and part of the drive to my conflicted nature, was a constant sense that I felt trapped. Having gotten an undergraduate degree in social work, I felt my understanding superseded some aspects of the program. I feel I was able to relate to the staff on a deeper and relational level than most of the residents. This may have justified being given privileges at an earlier time than I was. Perhaps I might have some remaining pride surrounding this issue.

DAY 84

I made it to morning meditation, and then made it back down to the facility for a group led by Christopher. I wasn't a big fan of this group. He had us read from a book about America's financial crisis. I am in complete agreement that we are in big trouble on the financial front. However, Christopher tried to make the case that this is a sign of the end of the world, and a sign of Christ's return. He also made a stance that this financial crisis is bringing about the New World Order and how it is a Biblical warning. I am not a fan of such apocalyptic worrying and fear. Instead, I desire to live my life for God, and let him take care of the rest. I'm not going to live in a perpetual state of fear and start stockpiling food in the belief that something drastic is going to happen. Christopher, however, feels we should start doing this.

THERE ARE SOME ASPECTS of Christianity that really get on my nerves now that I have deconstructed a lot of my old beliefs. The "End Times" is a topic at the top of the list of things continuing to annoy me about evangelicalism. From the Left Behind Series (frequently promoted at NH), to this "prophetic" lecture from Christopher, my bullshit bar was reaching an all-time high. I could take a lot, which I think is shown in my previous entries, but I do have a limit. From fundamental Christian revivals to religious cults, end times prophecies have been proclaimed for thousands of years. None of these so-called prophecies, however, have come to fruition. These scare tactics were increased and intensified in the U.S. with the release of the Left Behind Series. Either way, I was thoroughly shocked that even Christopher would stoop to this level of low hanging spiritual fruit.

DAY 86

Christopher called this morning to inform me that he would prefer I be in groups today and to not go with Matthew for the food ministry. This is my last week at this facility, and I absolutely love going out, especially since I'm leaving. Now, I'm stuck at the facility, and don't get to go anywhere. I came down to the facility with Marvin. Christopher had brought a guest to participate in groups. The guy was nice, but I found it very hard to pay attention since I wanted to be out with Matthew. Christopher's group was more on the American financial crisis. As I had suspected, Christopher had us do that topic for our second group as well.

I know I don't have much time left, but I seriously disagree with this topic. It's the biggest waste of time ever. Christopher is turning into a Christian end-times fanatic. He wants the house to begin collecting food and preparing for something drastic to happen in our economy and in the world. It's insane. I can't believe it. There are television shows about people like him, crying out loud! This is the kind of stuff people make fun of, and makes non-Christians scared of us. I want to have absolutely no part in any of this. The group was like pulling teeth, and I was bottled with anger. I was supposed to be out transitioning to leaving! Instead, I'm sitting in a group meant to instill fear, hoarding, and fundamentalism. I am furious!

I'VE MENTIONED THIS BEFORE, but Christopher was truly a loose cannon. He ran his life based on what seemed like the direction of the wind, making decisions that were almost always absolutely unpredictable. I've also previously mentioned that NH didn't always provide us with recovery-related material in our groups and meetings. It seemed the bar for what was proper for us to engage in, was whether it was "Christian" or not Christian. As a therapist looking back, I couldn't disagree with this approach any more adamantly than I do. Treatment should be geared toward, and focused on, *present* issues. Even if the program is based on religion, the religious material should be used *in combination* with the recovery curriculum—not alone. To supply religious material without any recovery component is not treatment but is like being in church (or worse, Sunday School). My parents weren't paying for me to go to church at NH, but to receive treatment for very real, and very serious mental health and substance abuse issues. End statement.

> Christopher asked me to lead Discipleship. I agreed and was happy to lead because it got me out of my slump. I appreciate being able to speak in front of the guys. Towards the end of the lesson, I shared one of the toughest things in following Christ. Christopher said I nailed it on the head, and then shared that he doesn't feel I am to that point. He asked the guys in the group and many shared that they fear I do not currently have the integrity to do what it takes to live a heterosexual life. I couldn't believe it. I'm leaving in four days and I should be feeling confident and excited about leaving. The brothers here should be encouraging me, and proud of me for the work I have done in my life. Instead, they are expressing concern about my readiness to leave.

> I found this entire thing confusing. I have sat down with Katherine in the last week and received confirmation about my departure. Then Katherine's husband confronts me in a

group and tells me he doesn't think I am ready—he doubts I have the integrity to live out a changed life. Do Katherine and Christopher not communicate with each other? Katherine personally knows me, and gives me thumbs up, while her husband barely knows me, and gives me thumbs down. I wish these two would get on the same page, because being told opposite things (especially receiving the negative in front of the guys), is upsetting and discouraging.

I feel I'm ready. I'm confident of where I stand. I am excited to spend time with my parents and to move on. Why are the people around me saying the opposite? I'm starting to feel uneasy. This is upsetting me. After hearing the guys express this concern, doubt is settling inside me. I want to scream and prove them wrong! I am confident in my integrity and am certain of the type of life I am going to live. Now, it seems I must prove that to Marvin and the rest. If I am unable to succeed in this, I guess I will just have to settle with it. I don't need the approval or validation from anyone else. I have a relationship with God and have the tools necessary to move forward. That's all I really need: God and tools.

I got out of the house as soon as I could. I really wanted some alone time. I value the walk back and forth from the facility to the house so much. It's about three blocks. I got home, brewed some coffee, and sat down in front of the TV. I decided to not eat supper. I spent an hour or so of my free time watching a special about Microsoft and Ian Allen. It was entertaining and informative. I enjoyed getting my mind off things for a little while.

I don't want to make rash assumptions regarding people's intentions. However, learning that the facility was low on cash, while subsequently asking me to stay another month seemed to be a bit more than mere coincidence. Having said that, it may not have been. Christopher could have genuinely been concerned for me, feeling as though the program had not worked for me. Deep down *I* knew it hadn't changed me and I believe Christopher and Katherine knew it too. The reason the program didn't work, however, was not related to the length of time I'd been at NH (or needing more time), but because the change I was originally seeking was *not possible*. Changing my sexuality simply was not going to work through prayer and dedication to Jesus. I had tried, and had tried, and had tried to change, based on recommendations given to me by others. But the promised change simply was *not going to happen*. Probably because it was never meant to.

DAY 87

Christopher took us to a beautiful park in the mountains. The park was at a lake surrounded by snow-covered mountains. I thought the area was breathtaking. Christopher had Kevin read a section out of Experiencing God about spending quiet time with the Lord, and then he set us free to roam the park and meet with God. I took a trail around the lake and then hiked up a bit into the mountains. I found a log that wasn't covered in snow and sat down. I had my iPod, so I played "My Desire" by Jeremy Camp. As I listened to this song, I began to pray for guidance and a word from God. I felt an overwhelming feeling that God loves me deeply, and I must continue in my task to be faithful in the small things. I also felt assurance and peace about my departure from this facility. A wave of peace came over me, and I knew that everything was going to be okay. I had successfully completed the task God had set before me by coming to this facility. Now, it was time to move on.

I was encouraged by the word from God, and it was what I'd needed to hear. Having received this assurance from God, I ended my time in prayer, and walked back to the van. I found Christopher sitting in the van and decided to confront him over yesterday's group. I shared with him that I was discouraged by what he had to say in-group. Christopher, however, did not feel the need to ease my discouragement, but continued in his attitude from yesterday. He shared that he was proud of my willingness to face the issues I have, but I must be extremely careful to not become arrogant and prideful. I was shocked at Christopher's demeanor and the confidence he held behind his criticism. I agree that there are areas I must work on, but why is he drilling me with such negativity just before my departure? I think he may be trying to shake me up in order to test my stability. If that is the case, I am perfectly okay with it. If, however, he is sincerely expressing concern and suggesting that I'm not ready to leave, I am disappointed.

We arrived back at the facility. As soon as we arrived, Christopher took one look around the facility and became angry, saying it wasn't clean enough for his standards. This didn't surprise me at all. Hunter was the king of cleaning within the facility, and now that he had left, I knew there would need to be a shockwave to awaken the guys to their increased responsibilities. It felt weird to be there as Christopher went around and criticized the guys' work. Since I am no longer living there, this criticism wasn't for me. However, I felt I should do something. Christopher went down to my house to get a mop. I planted myself in the kitchen to work photo editing while the guys cleaned.

When I walked back to my place, I found a note from Christopher on the counter. It read: "Seth, please clean house: 1) throw trash out 2) clean kitchen 3) sweep floor." He must have noticed that my house wasn't up to par as well when he came to get the mop. I stepped outside to have a cigarette and found Marvin and Mike also enjoying a smoke. They informed me that Christopher had come over and he was furious. I asked if it was about my house. They shared that Christopher had gotten into one of his moods and that yes, he was upset that I hadn't thrown out the cardboard boxes that were sitting on the counter. Marvin and Mike said not to take it personally. When Christopher gets upset, one should not take anything personally, but re-

alize that Christopher can be a loose cannon and shoot off at anyone or anything that doesn't meet his standards. Given my recent conversations with him, I took note of that trait. I have decided not to take it personally.

I came back inside and began cleaning. Marvin and Mike came over and helped me clean up. They stated everything looks good, and that I have nothing to worry about. I found that reassuring as I now have less than forty-eight hours here, and I don't want to create any unnecessary waves of conflict. I plan to scrub the kitchen counters tomorrow as an extra measure of precaution.

———◦———

CHRISTOPHER'S DESCRIBED BEHAVIORS IN this day's entry did not surprise me too much, but they *did* disappoint me. Like I've mentioned many times, Christopher tended to be a loose cannon with a short fuse. When he felt that something in his mind needed to be done, he wanted it done his way and right away. If it wasn't done his way he would become extremely upset and act like an injustice had been committed against him. Given how hard I'd worked in this program—that the house I was living in was mostly spotless, Christopher's behavior was discouraging. He treated me like I was living in utter chaos, when in fact, the trash simply needed to be taken out. His reaction was not appropriate to the situation. While I found this off-putting, I wasn't that surprised. It was after all, Christopher.

DAY 88

Katherine arrived at the facility. She called me into the office, and we had a decent conversation. She ran through my exit plan, and I needed to change a few things. I had figured this to be true, which was why I turned it in early. I wanted feedback. We also discussed the plans I have set for when I move home— the importance of having tight accountability and mentorship in place. Katherine described such an accountability system as being like the cement blocks along the highway. They serve to keep me on the road and prevent me from veering off track. The conversation was short, and it would be one of our last talks. I may get to speak privately to her again tomorrow just before I leave. Therefore, I was also able to discuss anything and everything on my mind. It was so nice to get things off my chest and clear the air. Katherine brings a wave of peace and tranquility over me. I was so very happy to meet and talk with her.

WHILE I WAS UPSET with how Christopher acted and responded to me, he also acted in same manner toward the guys at the main house (if not worse). I then felt it would have been wrong and selfish to bring up my concerns about Christopher with Katherine. Further, I was on my way out of the program, so I felt there was no need to raise hell before I left.

I did not address the ways which Christopher had hurt my feelings by criticizing my house (for having not taken out the trash).

By the time Katherine and I were done talking, it was almost time for my graduation. Several people came from Sober Living. Of these individuals, Marvin came, which meant a lot to me. I was a little nervous he wouldn't make it. Christopher started the graduation by reading a poem that seemed to apply to me well. From there, the guys went around the room, and spoke encouraging things about my life. I thought it was great to hear such encouragement, but I was sitting on the edge of my seat when it came to Katherine. She decided to sit next to me and brought me Starbucks. She shared that it had been an honor to spend time with me, and she looked forward to every minute of conversation that she was able to have with me—even when I was a messed up, arrogant, prideful manipulator. It's hard to express how lucky I feel to have people like this in my life, people who have refused to give up on me, even when I have given them reason to give up. The graduation was a great reminder of who I used to be, and who I am now.

Did you notice that a certain staff member was missing at my graduation from NH? I was surprised when Jackie didn't show up to be present on the big day. On one level, I can understand her absence, given that she didn't work at the facility every day. She likely had other responsibilities, but it was hard not to feel like I had been a special case. For all that I had gone through in her New Hearts ministry to try to change my sexuality, her presence at my graduation would at least have been supportive. Without her presence my graduation felt incomplete.

I don't have much time tomorrow, and I have lots to get done. Video for Christopher, cleaning the house, and packing. I was given the day off and didn't have to go to church. I arrived back at my house where I sat everything to the side for a while. I went outside on the back porch and smoked a cigarette. I couldn't believe it had all come down to this. There have been so many days I felt like I would never leave NH, but now, it seems like time has gone by so quickly. This place has impacted me in a profound way. I'm unsure if it will have the effect on my future life that I originally hoped for, but having said that, I am sure I won't be the same.

Before leaving the facility, I was given my cell phone. It felt weird having it with me, as I haven't been given such privileges since I've been here. Therefore, I felt the privilege shouldn't be taken lightly. I sat in the living room of the house and called several people. I called my parents, my brother, my cousins, and even Knives and Ethan. The conversations were short and really had no objective other than exercising my newfound freedom. Afterward, I sat at the kitchen counter and finished editing pictures. It was a joy to look through the pictures that had been taken at my graduation.

Being in the house alone at this point felt a bit strange. I went around cleaning as I saw fit and began packing everything from my three months here into my small suitcase.

Now that you've reached the end of me being at NH, I should level about my mental and emotional state as I was about to leave.

While I do not believe that any efforts I put into this program resulted in an effective sexual orientation change, I felt committed to the changes I'd promised to live by as I left. I didn't want this entire program to be for naught. I mean, my parents had spent a *lot* of money to try to make this work. The work I'd done included me becoming straight. I had dedicated three months to trying to change. Obviously, NH's program was not effective for me, and had only succeeded in instilling further shame and guilt. I honestly thought my time there caused me more harm than good. However, I believe that to make sense of my experience, I lied to myself. This was proven in the fact that later in graduate school, I would do clinical research to try to prove that sexual orientation change programs could be effective. I seriously grasped at every straw I could find.

The results of my treatment for substance use, however, had better, more successful outcomes. I do think that the facility was effective at training me to no longer want to engage in substance use behaviors on a frequent basis. I left the facility committed to no more unhealthy use of substances, whether that was alcohol (or anything else for that matter). I truly was committed to living a changed life. A health condition would later pop up in life, which made use of substances (specifically alcohol) problematic and something I rarely do anymore.

Spiritually, I had never felt closer to God than when I left NH. Hell, I'd never felt as close to God at any other point *in my life*! Who has time to dedicate twenty-four hours a day to spiritual growth (unless you happen to be a monk, but even then...). Summed up, I left this program with feelings that were both good and bad.

EPILOGUE

I woke up this morning feeling refreshed and excited. There was a rock in my stomach, showing my anxiety and nervousness. I couldn't believe this period in my life was all over. As a result, I was slow in getting my stuff together. I walked through the house and gave the place one last look. I sat my packed-up luggage by the door and met Marvin outside to walk down to the facility.

I was able to have one last group with Bob. The group centered around the stages of relapse. I honestly wasn't paying much attention—I was ready to leave. As his group finished, he asked all the guys to pray for me. I shuffled to the middle of the room, and all the guys placed their hands on my back while Bob prayed one last prayer for my safety and the anticipated change in my life.

Christopher walked in during this prayer so as soon as we were finished, he escorted me out the door to his truck. We picked up my stuff at the other house, and we were off to the airport. Along the way, I mentioned my previous girlfriend, Jennifer. As I was explaining the dynamics of our past relationship, she called me on my cell phone. Christopher later remarked that it was a "sign." I laughed and smiled.

Christopher dropped me off at the airport. We took a few pictures outside. After he left, I checked in my bags and

*waited for my flight. In a matter of thirty minutes, I was
up in the air and headed back home. I was unsure of what
would come next, but excited to experience normal life.*

———◦———

I NOW LOOK BACK at this entire experience with different colored glasses. I am no longer the person I was then. I view my experience at NH as traumatic overall, and my time there left me forced to shut down to survive. This is not to say I didn't learn anything about human behavior, or myself, because I did.

At NH I learned that other people, even when acting through the best of intentions, can cause great harm. The staff and other clients had no ill intent (of which they were aware) towards me or anyone else. They genuinely thought they were helping me. The byproducts of the "lessons" they instilled, however, further perpetuated my shame and guilt rather than giving me a means by which to alleviate the shame and guilt I'd already experienced. It has taken me *years* to move past the trauma of my time in the program. Constant and pervasive guilt is something I continue to deal with to this day and it has not been easily shaken off. Part of why I've shared this journal is so others can witness my day-to-day thought processes throughout my experience. I found it was beneficial for me to process through my life each day and it is my hope that you've found it insightful and helpful in your own journey.

After completing NH's program, I was still *very* confused about my sexuality. On one hand, I wanted to prove the steps I took in California had changed me "for the better"—that the time spent there had served its purpose. My family hadn't sent me away paying thousands of dollars for me to obtain no real result. On the other hand I felt driven to live of authenticity. This meant coming to accept myself for who I was then and am now. As a result, the internal conflict from the time at NH and thereafter did not resolve, but deepened instead. I used my graduate program in Social Work as a means to explore and analyze this internal conflict. I wrote many of my research papers to research and examine human sexuality and religion. My capstone research project was initially entitled *"The Effectiveness of Sexual Orientation Change Efforts/Reparative Therapy"* but later changed it to *"The Personal and Social Dynamics of a Sample of Men Who Identify as Homosexual."* The results of my study investigated seven different themes including personal stories, experiences with family, experiences with family/friends, sexual behavior, counseling related to sexual orientation issues, religious belief and views towards equality. My study analyzed these seven areas and drew correlations and similarities between these factors.

After completing graduate school, holding down a job became a struggle. I was still trying to operate in a state of shame and guilt, and this negativity bled into the workplace. I experienced a deep sense of insecurity and had porous boundaries with colleagues at work. I'd landed a well-paying job right out of grad school, which seemed like a big deal due to the impressive salary. With a big salary, however, comes big responsibility. I struggled to keep up with my job duties. I also found myself oversharing aspects from my gay conversion journey with my colleagues. Through this oversharing, lines were crossed, and interactions became uncomfortable for everyone. Not everyone agreed with what I had decided to do, and tension in my working relationships arose as a result. Regardless of the relationships with my colleagues, I was forced to quit my position after I experienced a grand mal seizure on Christmas Day of 2013. I previously had been completely unaware that the car accident at age six had left me at risk of having seizures. No doctors or specialists had ever even talked to me or my parents about having a traumatic brain injury (TBI). My family and I quickly learned that my TBI had resulted in epilepsy. Due to this seizure, I was unable to drive for six months, and was consequently forced to resign from my job.

I underwent a string of various employment endeavors, working in a variety of positions in an assortment of occupational settings. I worked as a crisis intervention clinician for a crisis line, care manager for an insurance company, a clinical trainer for a software company, a therapist in a crisis center, and now am a clinical supervisor and therapist for a private practice. It took a long time before I was finally able to settle down into a position that made sense.

Regarding the sexual orientation I'd tried so hard to "fix," I officially came out of the closet the day gay marriage was legalized in the United States—July 2, 2015. That day I found myself exasperated by the situation I was in. When the news of the legalization dropped, the thought that kept running through my head was "Wouldn't the God I believe in prefer I am honest about being gay than no longer here on earth?" I hadn't exactly been experiencing suicidal ideation at that time but suspected that if I continued down that current path, suicide would be the only logical outcome. That day I sat down and wrote a bold and straightforward Facebook post in which I came out of the closet. Due to our enmeshment, of course I told my parents. After they were notified, my parents requested I take my post down and call a list of close family and friends. In contacting people, I was to inform them that:

1) I was coming out of the closet as gay
2) I was going to come out publicly on Facebook and
3) if they have a problem seeing my posts moving forward, they have permission to unfriend me with no hard feelings.

It's possible my parents gave me this challenge as a bluff, thinking I would not be willing to follow through with these difficult conversations. I don't think my parents realized my exacerbation had reached a tipping point. I wasn't going to let anything get in my way. I called my parents' bluff and reached out to each family member and friend on their list. The amount of confrontation in each ensuing conversation varied from person to person. Some individuals were shocked that I would do this to my parents, some expressed surprise and confusion given my strong religious convictions, and others supported my decision to be true to myself and to own my future. Obviously, this all left me emotionally drained.

I then took the next step and reposted my Facebook post. At the time, I felt quite proud of myself for all I had done to fully come out of the closet. It cemented the event in time (kind of like saying the old sinner's prayer or getting baptized), and I finally felt I was able to do so with my character upheld. My second "coming out" Facebook post on July 2, 2015, said the following:

So let's try this again. Out of respect, I have called family and friends to inform them that I will be coming out on Facebook. Now that they have been contacted, it's time to make this official.

As many of you know, my faith has been very important to me. In fact, I wanted to pursue ministry at one point. However, upon learning that I had same-sex attraction- I chose social work instead.

My religious convictions have made my journey towards self acceptance a rough road. Based on my convictions, I received reparative therapy (to make me straight) in CA for three months. Unfortunately, no matter what I did-these feelings and attractions would not go away. The therapy's failure caused wreckage to my life: including increased depression, difficulty in employment and substance abuse issues. I wasn't just gay- I felt like I was a "failed Christian" because God hasn't changed me. Over time, however, I have come to realize that God loves me just as I am and that I do not need to change for anyone.

I'm finally taking a stand and owning up to who I am as a person. I am proud of who I am. I no longer want to hide. I no longer want to pretend to be someone I'm not. I am gay. I hope to someday date a man, get married and raise a family. Oh... And I am also still a Christian and love Christ (in case any of you wondered).

I understand many of you will have disagreements and potentially want to condemn me to hell. I understand your views and why you believe them. I respect you enough to ask that you simply delete or unfollow me if you have a problem with who I am or the things I post.

This is my official coming out post.

I was a bit dramatic with the line about "condemning me to hell" but at the time it felt right. There was a sense of satisfaction in officially coming out on Facebook (the most formal way I knew how in this technological era). My mention of Hell was a call-out to all the traumatic events about which you've just read. I didn't haphazardly just come out of the closet. Prior to doing so, I had committed my life to try and:

1) understand why I had same-sex attraction and
2) change my same-sex attraction to heterosexual attraction.

There has been a direct correlation between my faith in God and my acceptance of my homosexuality, probably not for the reasons you'd think. It's not that being gay was the antithesis of spirituality. It's not. In fact, I know many gay Christians.

Looking back at my years growing up, as well as my time at NH, I had been made so many promises by Christians—offered so much hope. In the end however, I found these promises to be based on a contrived ideal, rather than reality. Hyped-up spirituality with an over-disciplined lifestyle as was required at NH didn't lead to any kind of change. It instead led to utter depression and further isolation. My experiences with The Church were linked to my past desires to want to change, so it's hard for me to engage with anything related to Christianity without experiencing deep and overwhelming feelings of shame. These feelings, in essence, are the opposite of Christ's message of love. I am currently in *real* therapy, and my views on God are something I have been exploring. At this point in my journey, I am finding solace in my relationship with Christ, but avoid religious institutions. I see the Bible as having many words of wisdom, but I do not regard it as the one and true literal "Word of God".

You may be surprised to learn that I've had a very lonely, single gay life thus far. For all my writing and reflections about celibacy vs. gay marriage, a long-term relationship has never presented itself. For many years (even after my time in California), I did continue to engage in promiscuous behavior as a way to deal with my strong sex drive. However, over time, my interest in such activities has diminished. My relationship with George was the closest to a real romantic relationship I have experienced to date. At this point, I've lived alone for so long, I'm uncertain I'd want to bring another person into my space. I wouldn't call myself "celibate" as I don't limit opportunities for sexual encounters from time to time. I do, however, live a semi-celibate lifestyle. I spend ninety five percent of my time alone unless I'm at work, and rarely seek out dates or sexual escapades like I used to.

Despite the lack of success I had in altering my sexuality, I do feel there were some beneficial results from my time at NH. When I started my time there, I had been using drugs and alcohol as a way of coping with my internal guilt and shame. The program offered me skills to remain sober and provided psychoeducation regarding alcoholism. It's important to remember I attended the program for two reasons, sexual orientation change and substance use treatment. I had started using substances as a way of functioning, having the overwhelming sense that I was a failure and not good enough. The impact of trying to change my sexual orientation was lasting damage; however, there had been good results from the counseling I received for substance use. A long time being far away from an environment which had encouraged substance abuse including negative influences in my life, made a significant difference in my perspective in the following years. Further, given the spiritual components of the program, I was in a constant state of contemplation at NH. I was forced to take things more seriously and to heart. After leaving the program, I felt much more levelheaded. I still struggled with my mental health and the trauma caused by my experience but wasn't nearly as risky in my experiential avoidance.

I must say, the sexual orientation change efforts administered by NH's staff weren't that intense compared to others I've heard about. I spent time with a sex therapist, a spiritual guru, and a Focus on the Family textbook, but all-in-all, I've heard worse cases. Having said this, trauma is in the eye of the beholder. And well, this experience *was* traumatic for me. Traumatic in that I had been told to place complete trust and confidence in a belief that not only was God real, but that He was *personally* invested in helping me change my sexual orientation. All the groups, lessons, and therapy I underwent through NH's program boiled down to one thing: *everything was on me, but I couldn't take credit for anything I did that was good.* In essence, I was given the message that if I didn't succeed in changing my sexual orientation, I simply wasn't strong enough in my faith and relationship with God. I one hundred percent bought into the message that I was at fault for all my "bad," and God was responsible for any of my "good." The consequent shame and guilt following my lack of "success" were far too much to bear and were what eventually led me out of the closet.

The treatment center that in this book I have referred to as "NH" is no longer in business. The only people I have stayed in touch with over the years are the owners of the facility, "Katherine" and "Christopher." After finishing the program, I ended up aiding them in developing a new website. I provided pictures from my stay and created a short video highlighting features of their program. Additionally, I have reached out to Katherine a few times over the years. One example of my reaching out was when I was quite upset after finding out I had lost a friend to suicide. I reached out to Katherine for support, thinking that given our history, I could speak candidly with her. Unfortunately, I found the opposite to be true. She made it clear she did not support my lifestyle, nor did she approve of my life choices, but she was sorry for what I was going through. Her hollow "caring" voice was telling.

As I've been re-reading this journal and adding my reflections I have been quite taken aback by how much I actually went through at NH and have overcome since. Who I am now is so different. It's quite amazing when I think about it. To answer the question of whether I'm happy with my life in the present-day while writing this epilogue, I immediately thought of my employment. This is somewhat telling. As a mental health professional, I have made my job *my life*. This is not a healthy practice, and I know it. However, when I consistently strive in serving the needs of others, a healthy relationship with work is a struggle. I do think that I am trully happy, though. Could I be happier, sure! Who couldn't? And trust me, I'm not one to be shy about what I think needs to change or what I need to have in order for my life to be better. I could write an entire book. Happiness is not the point of it all, though. Happiness is not about having everything going your way, but having life work in a manageable, routine, and familiar way—being able to meet one's basic needs.

Regarding my mental health, depression is still a real struggle. Thank you so much for that, TBI! It is quite ironic but true of the mental health profession—most mental health professionals have mental health disorders. Many of us go into this field to first try to resolve our own mental health conflicts, but then fall in love with serving and helping others. I might even say that many of the best mental health providers are those who have faced darkness themselves. It's in fighting our own struggles that we learn to help others through theirs. It's through the rough terrain of our experiences that my colleagues and I are uniquely qualified to delve into the depths of people's hearts and minds. My main takeaway here is that I believe that my experience at NH prepared me to do the work I do today. I do not believe that I would have the empathy or ability to relate to others, had it not been for the trauma I endured.

Conversely, my relationship with my parents has improved tenfold over the years. They have truly come a long way in accepting the sexualities of my brother and me. While they still attend The Church I went to in college (which is a source of contention with me), they accept my brother and I for who we are as individuals. They have no expectation that we will change this aspect of ourselves. My brother is now engaged to be married to a Black man who I absolutely adore. My parents welcomed him into our family with open arms and have even allowed my brother and his partner to sleep in the same room when they stay over during holiday events. I know that for my parents, this transformation has not been an easy one. Reconciling their crises of faith, while continuing to attend a Church which remains publicly anti-LGBTQIA+, hasn't been an easy path to tread. However, somehow my parents have been able to do so. For their love and acceptance, I am exceedingly grateful.

I want to discuss a big "what not to do" revelation from my experience at NH (as well as to mental health in general). I strongly recommend trying to *not* make decisions in the heat of the moment, and to seek outside advice before making life-changing decisions. When I think back to how this all got started, when I was crying out to my parents for help, I was experiencing same-sex attraction. However, my belief was that my same-sex attraction was inherently wrong. This internal conflict had driven me directly into substance use, and I was making very unwise decisions. I came up with the idea of undergoing a gay conversion program as a Hail Mary, or a *"Let's see what they'll say to this,"* idea, if you will. I was in a state of utter desperation and didn't know what to do with myself. When my parents agreed I needed help, I was ready to strap in and go for the ride (even against my brother's misgivings). Looking back, I wish I had consulted with an outpatient therapist *before* making this huge decision.

I feel compelled to include a statement directed toward the world of Evangelical Christianity (aka., "The Church")—the promises that were made to me, how I am feeling now.

I have made many life-altering decisions based on tenants and beliefs set forth by the contemporary Church. Let me be clear—I know not all churches treat their LGBTQIA+ members or attendees the way I was treated. I speak in terms of The Church as a whole.

It is my hope in writing this book, my heart and intentions have been clear. I have *genuinely* and *sincerely* followed through on what multiple Evangelical churches and organizations have told me to do in all aspects of my life—the right way to live (not only pertaining to sexuality), from childhood until the day I left for NH. *I* had been the one who asked to go away to NH—not my parents, nor anyone else for that matter. I fervently requested gay conversion therapy because of my faith in what I had been told. And I had been told that if I didn't repent, I would go to Hell, cutting myself off from the love of God for all eternity. Hearing that over and over again was really its own Hell in and of itself, but I didn't know it at the time.

This journal obviously contained an excess of the back-and-forth internal conflict I constantly put myself through. For a long time though, I'd made all my decisions based on recommendations and promises offered by The Church—its leaders, its members, its counselors, all the individuals from whom I'd sought help. When I was unsuccessful at changing my sexual orientation, I ultimately recognized self-acceptance was what I had needed to embrace all along. Realizing that God loves me, even when The Church has chosen not to accept me for who I am, has been one of (if not *the most*) freeing and fulfilling insights of my life.

However, there still remains a deep part of me wanting some kind of an admission of wrongdoing (or at least some indication of regret) from those who emotionally controlled and manipulated me, failed me in their own promises, then rejected me. Most individuals who know me and are still involved in The Church (as well as the staff of NH) have remained firm in their stance toward me. I am just another failed case in their eyes—another poor unfortunate soul, destined for Hell. Most evangelicals look at me with pity, then turn their backs. Others choose to ignore the fact that I *am* gay, and pretend to "love the sinner, hate the sin." This is a ridiculously patronizing cliché by the way! (Speaking of, just let that line go, Christianity—if being gay is "just another sin" you shouldn't have so many difficulties with transgender issues, either. Obviously deep-down people know gender and issues of sexuality involve more than just "choosing to live in sin". By coming out, members of LGBTQIA+ community aren't just having a willy-nilly sexual hay day).

Over the years since my time at NH members of The Church have directly and indirectly told me that my lack of success in changing my sexual orientation is *my* fault. I have heard all their explanations why I was unsuccessful—I didn't have enough faith. I didn't pray hard enough. I didn't truly "surrender." According to The Church, *I alone* am to blame for my lack of change. However, The Church was the entity that originally told me I *should* and *could* be "fixed" in the first place. Shouldn't The Church be held accountable to the same standards to which it holds nonbelievers? Shouldn't The Church live as an example of love, compassion, and humility? What was Christ's message?

To The Church, I ultimately want to say this—The reason you were unsuccessful in "fixing me," the reason I didn't magically become straight, the reason I didn't wake up one morning inspired to be celibate for the rest of my life was the plain and simple fact that ***there was no problem for you to fix***. God loves me for who I am. I firmly believe *He* didn't want or need me to change. This was the reason my earnest, tearful, and heartfelt pleas for Him to change me didn't "work." Being gay is *not a problem*. Being gay *does not equate sin*. Being *gay is part of who I am*. It is ok for you to embrace me, and others like me. It is ok for you to let people be who they are, for you to let them feel God's love, for you to let all people love whoever they love. It is ok to admit you might need to change your views. I definitely needed to change mine!

As a message for those who are reading this who are gay or may be experiencing same-sex attraction (but don't want to be gay due to religious teaching), please know this—you have worth and value exactly for who you are *right now*. I can sit here and try to encourage you against trying to change your sexuality, but in the end, it's your decision to make. No one can make that decision for you—not your family, not your friends, not your Church. Having said that, if there's anything I've learned through my journey, it's that surrender is required. Mine was not the surrender I had been expecting or had handed down to me as ***The Answer***. Rather, the surrender required was a *surrender to acceptance*: acceptance that I am gay and it's okay, accepting that being gay is okay with my God, and that He loves and accepts me exactly for who I am. There was no fault in my design. My struggle did not originate with a lack of surrender to God. It was a lack of surrender to authenticity. And since I've surrendered to authenticity, I am finally free. My once-fractured self is now whole again.

BIBLIOGRAPHY

CROSSWAY, *ESV STUDY BIBLE* (Wheaton, IL: Crossway, 2001), 2159.

Gilbert, Don. "15 Styles of Distorted Thinking." Publishing Date Unknown.

Revoice. "About—Revoice," n.d. Retrieved from https://www.revoice.org/about.

Solzhenitsyn, Aleksandr. 2018. *The Gulag Archipelago*. London, England: Vintage Classics.

Worthen, Frank. 1995, *Helping People Step Out of Homosexuality*. Grand Rapids, MI: Baker Book House.

END NOTES

BIBLIOGRAPHY

DAY 11

1 Romans 12:1.

DAY 12

1 2 Corinthians 10:5.

DAY 16

1 Solzhenitsyn, Aleksandr. 2018. The Gulag Archipelago. London, England: Vintage Classics.

DAY 21

1 Worthen, Frank. Helping People Step Out of Homosexuality. Grand Rapids, MI: Baker Book House, 1995.
2 Proverbs 22:6.

DAY 29

1 ESV Study Bible (Wheaton, IL: Crossway, 2008), 2199.

DAY 33

1 "15 Styles of Distorted Thinking." Dr. Don Gilbert. Undated. Retrieved from https://newlife-counseling.com/wp-content/uploads/2020/09/15-Styles-of-Distorted-Thinking.pdf.

DAY 58

1 Revoice. "About—Revoice," n.d. https://www.revoice.org/about.

For more information about Seth Showalter,
or to contact him for speaking engagements,
please visit www.SethShowalter.com.

Many Voices. One Message.

www.quoir.com

Made in the USA
Monee, IL
11 October 2023

44381424R00171